God's Will and Your Life

GOD'S WILL
AND
YOUR LIFE

T. B. Maston

BROADMAN PRESS • *Nashville, Tennessee*

Dewey Decimal classification number: 231
Library of Congress catalog card number: 64-10816
Printed in the United States of America
3.5AL6413

To
Eugene and Frieda

Preface

This book has been written primarily for Christian youth who are seeking the will of God for their lives. It is hoped that parents, pastors, and other counselors of young people will also find it helpful.

The discussions are limited to the will of God for the individual child of God. They will not include the broader aspects of the will of God—his will for the family, the church, the community, the nation, and human relations in general. But it should be kept in mind that God's will is inclusive of the totality of life. He is creatively active in every realm of life. He is no idle spectator. He is on the move in achieving his purposes in the world.

The approach will be quite personal. I have thought of these discussions as conversations with interested young people. This explains the prevalence of personal pronouns, the use of personal experiences, and the general writing style.

Many people have contributed, in varying ways, to the writing of this book. Through the years, young people have shared with me not only their problems in knowing the will of God but also their reactions to my ideas concerning the will of God. They have helped me to rethink and to clarify my viewpoints.

Appreciation is expressed to the following who have read and appraised the manuscript: Wayne Barnes, Jess Fletcher, Gordon Harris, Josephine Harris, Lloyd Householder, Bill

Junker, Bob Kilgore, Martha Newport, Bill Pinson, and Frances Whitworth. Their suggestions resulted in considerable revision and improvement of the manuscript. Our son Eugene and his wife Frieda have been unusually objective and helpful. I have taken the liberty to dedicate the book to them, a comparatively young couple who have already devoted several years to an intelligent and effective service to college youth.

Appreciation is also expressed to Macel Ezell and Mrs. Melvin Bridgford for the typing of the manuscript at its various stages.

Several versions of the Bible have been used, but unless otherwise indicated quoted Scripture passages are from the Revised Standard Version. The abbreviation KJV refers to the King James Version, and ASV to the American Standard Version.

T. B. MASTON

Contents

Part I

God's Will

1. His Will Applies to All 9
2. His Will Is Always Best 15
3. A Continuing Experience 21
4. Choosing Your Lifework 29
5. Choosing Your Life's Companion 37
6. Making Daily Decisions 43

Part II

How Can We Know God's Will?

7. Use Personal Resources 50
8. Seek Counsel of Others 56
9. Study the Bible 63
10. Pray 69
11. Respond to the Holy Spirit 75
12. Have a Willing Heart 79
13. Look Beyond the Problems 85

Part I: God's Will

1
His Will Applies to All

As we approach this study together, let us remember that God wants to start with each one of us where we are and guide us to where he wants us to go.

Are you willing to let God start with you where you are? Will you seek in every way possible to know his will? Will you keep your heart and mind open to the leadership of the Holy Spirit? Will you read these brief chapters carefully and prayerfully, asking our Heavenly Father to reveal to you his will and purpose for every area of your life?

The experience of mature Christians suggests that within all of us is an inner battle—the lower or carnal nature vs. the higher or spiritual nature. In a sense this is a conflict between our will, which is only partially redeemed, and God's will. Are you conscious of this conflict within your own soul? If you are, do not be surprised or discouraged by it. However, do not hopelessly surrender to the pull of the lower.

The call.—The initial call or invitation of Jesus was, and is, "Follow me." In the life of Peter these words came at the beginning (Mark 1:17), and also at the close, of his association with Jesus (John 21:22). This call or invitation to Peter and the other disciples of that day is the Master's call to every disciple of every day. It is his invitation to you and to me. It first comes to us in our salvation experience. Inherent in the experience is a call to follow Christ, to make his will and way first in our lives.

9

The call to follow him is not only his initial invitation, but, since none of us follows him as closely or perfectly as we should, it is also his continuing call or invitation. As we respond to this invitation of Jesus, we shall discover that it has much more depth and meaning than we had anticipated. We shall discover that it affects every area of our lives. We shall come to comprehend more fully that it means to walk in the way that Jesus himself walked, which was in complete obedience to the will of the Father. Here is enough to challenge us to the end of life's journey!

The commission.—Once we accept the call of Jesus, we shall find that the call becomes a command or a commission. The initial invitation of Jesus was, "Come, follow me"; his closing command was, "Go ye." The coming was, and is, preparatory to the going.

The so-called Great Commission (Matt. 28:18-20), which provides the marching orders for individual Christians, as well as churches, is the call of Christ to obedience to his purpose and plan for the winning of the world. An important part of that Commission is "teaching them to observe [to practice, Williams] all that I have commanded you." As disciples, we are commissioned not only to be obedient to his commands but also to teach others to be obedient.

After his resurrection, Jesus, on one occasion, stood in the midst of the inner circle of perplexed and fearful disciples and said to them: "Peace be unto you: as my Father hath sent me, even so send I you" (John 20:21, KJV). No verse of Scripture has gripped my own life any more in recent years than these words of the resurrected Christ.

He was sent; we are sent. He was sent into the world to do his Father's will; we are sent to do his will. He was sent to reveal the Father; we are sent to reveal him. He was God incarnate; we are to be Christ incarnate. He was sent to redeem man; we are sent to be a redeeming influence among men. We can and will reveal him and be a redeeming influence for him only as we follow him, only as we let him live in us and express himself through us.

The challenge.—Christ's call and commission challenge us to give our best and to be our best for him. He does not want any halfhearted followers. His counsel is, "Stop and count the cost. Unless you are willing to pay the price, you had better not start to follow me." No leader of men has ever presented a challenge equal to his.

Have we felt the challenge of his call? More important, have we responded? Christ commissions no unwilling recruits. He accepts only volunteers. If we have enlisted, then we should not be satisfied to be nominal, ordinary Christians. The cause of Christ is suffering from the mediocrity of many who claim to be his followers. We need to see more clearly that not only are we invited to accept Christ as Saviour, but we are also challenged to follow him as the Lord of our lives.

If Christ is our Lord, and he is if we are his followers, then we are his servants or slaves. Our supreme allegiance belongs to him. This means that every area of our lives must be open to him and to his control. Our bodies belong to him; we are to use them for his glory (cf. 1 Cor. 6:12-20). They are to be presented to him as "a living sacrifice" (Rom. 12:1). Our minds and our total personalities also belong to him and are to be dedicated to his will and purpose. We are to seek "first the kingdom of God" (Matt. 6:33); it is to be the pearl of great price, the treasure hid in the field for which we are to be willing to give up everything (cf. Matt. 13:44-46). This is his challenge! What is our response?

The cost.—If we take seriously the challenge to do the will of God, to seek first his kingdom, and to make Christ

the Lord of our lives, we shall discover, even in our day,
that the cost will be considerably more than most of us had
thought. This should not surprise us. Christ, who came to
do the Father's will, had to go to the cross by way of
Gethsemane. If we make God's will our will, if we walk in
the way that Jesus walked, it will take us to a cross, which
is the abiding symbol of voluntary redemptive self-denial
and self-sacrifice. Dietrich Bonhoeffer, a creative German
Christian who was slain by the Nazis during World War
II when he was less than forty, has rightly said that when
Jesus bids one come, he bids him come and die. In other
words, the cross is an integral part of the initial, as well as
the continuing, call or invitation of Jesus.

Bonhoeffer has also said that cheap grace is the bitterest
foe of all true discipleship. One evidence of this cheap
conception of grace is the attempt, entirely too prevalent,
to separate the saviorship of Christ from his lordship—a
separation which is impossible.

Many of us have a very limited conception of what it
means to be a disciple of Christ. A disciple is a student,
one who learns from his teacher. In the case of our Teacher
or Master, the best way to learn is to walk in the way he
walked—the way of self-denial and self-sacrifice. Over and
over again Jesus said that he had not come to do his own
will but the will of the one who had sent him.

The will of God was central in Jesus' life. It was, to use
an expression of John R. Mott, the "North Star" of his life.
His dedication to the will of the Father was climaxed in his
prayer in Gethsemane and in his death on the cross. In the
former he prayed, "My Father, if it be possible, let this cup
pass from me; nevertheless, not as I will, but as thou wilt"
(Matt. 26:39). Here is prayer at its highest and best. The
inner crucifixion was complete. He was ready for all that
lay immediately ahead.

The will of the Father was as fully accepted in the garden of Gethsemane as it was on the cross. If we walk in the way that Jesus walked, it will take us through Gethsemane to Calvary. We shall discover that the cross is not exclusively where Christ died "on a hill far away" but that it becomes a living experience in our own lives.

John Mills, a former student of mine, had caught something of the challenge in following Christ when he gave his testimony on Foreign Mission Night at the Southern Baptist Convention some years ago. He was a new appointee. His words thrilled me as they did thousands of others. "God has called me to Nigeria. There was a time when this field was called the graveyard of the missionaries." Then came the statement that has challenged me through the years: "I would rather go to Nigeria and not live out my first term of service, and know that I was in the center of the will of God, than to live threescore years and ten and be outside of his will." This should not only be the attitude of a missionary but of every child of God.

The results.—By now some of you may be saying, "I do not know many Christians who take seriously this matter of following Christ. I do not know many who deny self, who have taken up a cross to follow him. I do not know many John Millses." Unfortunately, this is true and it handicaps the cause of Christ more than anything else. So few of us live for him as we should.

Where are we in our walk with Christ? To make the question personal: How faithfully are you seeking to know and to do the will of God? Are you seeking his will in every area of your life, regardless of what others may say or do?

There are some glorious results that will flow from our willingness to do God's will, to co-operate with him in his purposes. As we do his will, we shall discover the most abiding joy and peace and the deepest sense of personal fulfilment. All of life will have a clearer sense of meaning, purpose, and direction.

Entrance into the kingdom or the rule or reign of God is conditioned on doing the Father's will (Matt. 7:21). Kinship to Jesus is based on doing the will of his Father, "for whoever does the will of my Father in heaven is my brother, and sister, and mother" (Matt. 12:50). Another glorious result is that the more obedient we are to him, the more we shall become like him. One purpose of God for our lives is that his image within us, which was marred by sin, should be restored through our union with Christ. This restoration will not be complete until the end of life's journey, when we shall awake in his likeness. However, we shall grow in our likeness to him as we walk with him in humble obedience.

The responsibility.—Our Heavenly Father has a will for us in every area of our lives, but we have the responsibility to respond to that will. This is both a wonderful and a terrible truth. It is wonderful in that we are free, but terrible to remember that we alone are responsible for what we do with that freedom. As maturing Christian individuals, we cannot shift this responsibility to our parents, our teachers, or our friends.

God respects the man he has created. He has given to him a will. He will not force or override that will, neither in the initial experience, when one becomes a child of God, nor in the continuing challenge of his call. Tennyson's *In Memoriam* refers to Christ as the perfect ideal of manhood:

> Thou seemest human and divine,
> The highest, holiest manhood, thou.
> Our wills are ours, we know not how;
> Our wills are ours, to make them thine.

How wonderful it would be if all of us could say with the psalmist, "I delight to do thy will" (40:8).

2

His Will Is Always Best

A missionary, speaking in chapel, told of the things that he and his family had given up in order to work among the people of a different culture and race. He then briefly reviewed some of the fruits and joys of their labors on the mission field—the unsaved who had been won to the Lord, the saved who had been trained, the gratitude of the people, and the joy in feeling that they were in the center of God's will for their lives. Then he made a statement that has stayed with me ever since:

"God has so ordered things that we cannot make a real sacrifice for him. He gives us so much in return for anything we give up for him that we see that we have not made a real sacrifice at all." It costs something to respond to the will of God, but it pays rich dividends.

Let me ask you two questions that are related, to some degree, to the preceding paragraph and to the remainder of this chapter: (1) What are the things you want most in life? (2) How do you think you will come nearer having these things—within or outside the will of God?

His will and our fulfilment.—We are referring here to the fulfilment of one's potentialities. How will you find the highest fulfilment of all of your possibilities? Not by seeking it directly, but by forgetting self, as within the will of God you serve your fellowman.

What has been true in my life, I think, is true in the lives of others. I believe that I have found the fullest expression for whatever talents I may have in the field of theological education. For years I have interpreted this to be the will of God for my life. God does not make any mistakes. His will is always best for us, as well as for his cause. This is true not only in the area of one's lifework but in every other area of life.

His will and our freedom.—The desire for freedom is one of the deepest desires of the human spirit. This hunger for freedom, which helps to explain the contemporary restlessness of the masses of the world, is particularly prevalent among young people. You want to be free from restraining restrictions. You tend to chafe under rules and regulations. Rather paradoxically but explainably, some who are most vocal in their desire for freedom from adult control, and even adult influence, are largely dominated or enslaved by their own age group or their particular crowd. The crowd determines how they dress, the music they listen to, the books and magazines they read, the places they go, and their activities and moral standards in general.

Whether or not the latter is true of you, you do seek freedom. Will you really find it by throwing off every restraint? Is there a distinction between liberty and license? Can one become enslaved to the lack of restraint?

How does a child of God find his fullest freedom? He finds it within the will of God. Does this will restrain him at times from doing things he might like to do? The answer quite evidently is yes. But God never expects a child of his to give up anything that is best for him. One becomes free, in the truest sense, by becoming a slave of Christ, by surrendering his will to God's will.

This is one of the glorious paradoxes of the gospel—freedom through enslavement. "If the Son makes you free, you will be free indeed" (John 8:36). Basically, the freedom referred to here is freedom from the enslavement of sin. This is the freedom we need most. The only way a Christian, as well as a non-Christian, can become free from the enslavement of sin is to become a slave of Christ and righteousness (cf. Rom. 6:12-23). Paul says, "Christ set us free, to be free men. Stand firm, then, and refuse to be tied to the yoke of slavery again" (Gal. 5:1, *The New English Bible*). Are you really free, or are you enslaved by what you have interpreted to be your freedom?

His will and our power.—Some men want to have power *over* other men; the real Christian wants to have power *with* men. He wants to influence them for good and God. The secret to this kind of power is in the presence of God, but we cannot have his presence unless we are walking within his will.

It was the resurrected Christ who said to his disciples, "Tarry ye in the city [Jerusalem], until ye be clothed with power from on high" (Luke 24:49, ASV). What was to be the source of that power? We find the answer in his words to them a little later: "Ye shall receive power, when the Holy Spirit is come upon you" (Acts 1:8, ASV).

What if they had not been obedient to him; what if they had not tarried in Jerusalem? The Spirit would not have come. They would not have had the power for a Pentecost.

Most of us are largely powerless in our lives because we have not learned to tarry until the power comes. The tarrying in meditation and prayer is just as much a command of our Lord as the testifying or witnessing. We need to remember that spiritual power is not, nor can it be, manufactured *by* or *within* us; it is released *through* us. It can be released, however, only through obedient hearts and lives. What tremendous resources of unreleased power are available to all of us as children of God!

God will never expect us to do anything for which he will not give us the strength. He will give the power if we

will depend upon him for it. Many of you know this by
your own personal experiences. On occasions when you
were to speak, to teach, to sing, or to witness, you felt the
need for the Lord's help. You took the time to ask him
to give you the power and strength you needed. As a result, you felt his power flow into you and through you.
Other times you have not had a sense of need; you have
depended on your own wisdom and resources. As a result,
you knew within your own heart that you had largely
failed, regardless of what people may have thought. Knowing that we may have God's power, why do we so frequently fail to tarry in his presence until the power comes?

Let us remember the statement by Jesus, "Apart from
me you can do nothing" (John 15:5), and the one by Paul,
"I can do all things in him who strengthens me" (Phil.
4:13). Without Christ we can do nothing; with him we can
do anything that he expects us to do. Here is our hope and
our victory. A Christian who walks within God's will is like
a boat with its sails set just right for the wind, or a plane
flying in and with the jet stream. He has a power outside
himself that carries him along.

His will and our peace.—Do you remember the questions that were asked earlier in this chapter? One of them
was: "What are the things you want most?" Was peace one
of the things you wanted? Possibly not, but was "happiness"
on your list? It is closely related to peace, unless one has
a very superficial conception of happiness. There is no
real happiness without peace of mind and heart. And, there
can be no peace for the child of God when he is conscious
of being outside the will of God. It was Dante who said,
"In His will is our peace." Many Christians, both young
and old, can testify to the truthfulness of this statement.

Perhaps you have struggled over the will of God for your
life. When it finally becomes clear to you and you make

your decision to do his will, then you will have peace that you have not known before. The deepest and most meaningful peace that can come to any child of God is when he honestly and sincerely prays, "Not as I will, but as thou wilt" (Matt. 26:39). It can be his Gethsemane of victory. He discovers in that experience that the secret of the peace which passes all understanding (cf. Phil. 4:7) is in the consciousness of the presence of the resurrected Christ. And there can be no consciousness of his presence unless we walk in obedience to him. This applies not only to one's lifework but to daily decisions in every area of life.

His will and the laws of life.—All of life is governed by basic laws. The operation of these laws is more immediately evident in some areas than in others. One such area is health. If an individual wants to enjoy good health, he knows that he must learn the laws of health and conform to them. He knows that he may violate those laws and get by for a while, but sooner or later payday will come. In other words, the penalty for the violation of the basic laws of life is inherent in the laws themselves. This means that the penalty is inevitable, for "whatever a man sows, that he will also reap" (Gal. 6:7).

The great law of sowing and reaping can be a wonderful as well as a terrible thing. Paul not only said, "He who sows to his own flesh will from the flesh reap corruption;" but added, "He who sows to the Spirit will from the Spirit reap eternal life" (Gal. 6:8).

It is wise to remember that this law, which is an expression of the will of God, is for our good. This is true also of every formalized expression of the will of God as found in the basic moral laws of the Old Testament, as well as in the teachings of Jesus. For example, in Jesus' conflict with the Pharisees over the sabbath, he said that the sabbath was made for man and not man for the sabbath (cf. Mark 2:27). Every requirement or commandment of God is for man's benefit. His commandments are not burdensome (cf. 1 John 5:3). Do not forget that, in contrast, the pleasures of sin are fleeting or are for a season (Heb. 11:25, KJV), and in many cases it is a very short season.

Have you ever approached an old church building with huge stained glass windows? Those windows appeared dirty, dingy, and unattractive. But when you went into that church and looked at those same windows from the inside, you saw their majesty, their beauty, their reverent symbolism. One view was from the outside, the other, inside. This is a rather feeble illustration of the child of God and the will of God. His will frequently looks entirely different, once we are on the inside. That which was dark and foreboding becomes the most glorious thing in our lives.

Since God's will is always best for us, we should seek earnestly to know his will, and once we know it, we should not fight against it but do it joyously.

3

A Continuing Experience

God's will for your life and mine is a constantly enlarging, expanding experience. It is never static but always dynamic. It could not be otherwise since it includes the totality of our lives and is always an ideal of perfection. It includes what we are and what we do in every relation of life. It also includes what we think, feel, and will. God also has a will concerning our ambitions, purposes, and motives. His will is much broader and deeper than we realize.

Our limitations.—Because of our limitations, we cannot fully comprehend the will of God for our lives. Because this is true, God at times seems to adjust the revelation of his will to our capacity to understand it. We are his children but his very imperfect children.

Many of us are far more immature than we should be. We continue to be babes in Christ, when we should be mature, or at least maturing, men and women for Christ. The ultimate goal of our lives is the "perfect measure of Christ's moral stature" (Eph. 4:13, Williams). We all fall distressingly below that high standard! This means, among other things, that throughout our lives the will of God must be a progressive or continuing experience.

God's wisdom.—In contrast to our limitations, God is infinitely wise. His wisdom, as already implied, is proved by the fact that he does not seek to reveal his complete will to us in one dramatic experience. This was not even true for Saul on the Damascus road, and it has not been true of other great saints. If this was not true of them, we should not expect it to be true of us. God, in his wisdom, knows that the gradual unfolding of his will will be best for us. So, if you do not see all the way right now, do not fret and worry. Simply trust the Lord to give you additional insight when you need it.

God in his wisdom also knows that we mature as we depend upon him for guidance and strength. Since finding his will is a continuing experience or a continuing series of experiences in our lives, we have to return to him again and again for wisdom and strength. This is an important factor in our spiritual maturing. If we could see the will of God for our lives to the end of the way, we might be tempted to depend on ourselves rather than on God for the strength to do his will.

Many older Christians can testify that it would not have been best for them to have seen all the way they were to travel. They might not have had the faith and courage to respond favorably to the call of Christ. Like the rich young ruler, they might have turned away and thus have missed the glorious blessings of fellowship with him.

We know that the deeper blessings of that fellowship come only to those who in faith walk with him from Gethsemane to Golgotha. But the cross is only for the mature. Thank God, however, some of the most mature spiritually are young in years. Some are more willing to deny self and take up a cross than many of us who are much older. I trust that you are in this group.

Someone has suggested that in seeking to reveal himself and his will to Israel God led her by the hand as a nurse would lead a child. In this way the children of Israel came to understand more clearly his purpose for them. In the same way, God wants to lead us in the paths of moral and spiritual maturity. He wants to lead us to a fuller understanding of and a more complete dedication to his will. He will lead. Will we follow?

The direction of our lives.—None of us is fully co-operative with the will of God. To be so would mean to be perfect. The test of our lives is not whether or not we are perfect but rather, are we moving in the direction of perfection? Are we making progress in our commitment to the will of God? Do we understand and co-operate more fully with his will today than we did yesterday, this week than last week, this month than last month, this year than last year? God judges our lives not so much by where we are as by where we are going; and, possibly we should add, by the speed with which we are moving in that direction.

Let us return for a moment to a consideration of the step-by-step leadership of the Lord, which is the way he works in most of our lives. Some of us are impatient; we want to see far down the road. We need to accept the fact that we do not know for sure where the road we are on will lead. The main question is, are we on the right road now, are we walking within his will today? If we are, we can trust him for the succeeding tomorrows.

The best assurance of light for tomorrow's decisions is to walk in the light of his truth and will today. Remember the old Chinese proverb, "A journey of a thousand miles begins with one step." Will you take that step? The airliner gets to its destination, not by seeing all the way before it starts, but by following "the beam." Are you on the beam of God's will now? Will you keep on that beam? If so, you will ultimately reach God's destination for your life.

When disappointment comes.—What can and should you do when something happens in your life that seemingly prevents your doing what you have interpreted to be the will of God? Does God have a will for you under such circumstances? Possibly we should ask a prior question: Is such an interruption or change of plans included within the will of God?

It is doubtful if we, with our human limitations, can ever fully comprehend the intentional or perfect will of God, or that we can be sure about the distinction between the intentional and the circumstantial will of God. It may be that the best we can do is to know, with relative certainty, what God's will is for us under the immediate circumstances. If this is true, then we can trust that if we are obedient to our Heavenly Father now this obedience will move us in the direction of his perfect or intentional will.

It is possible, as implied previously, that many of the incidents that change the evident direction of our lives are expressions of God's circumstantial or permissive will but not necessarily a part of his intentional or perfect will. For example, a father's death may make it necessary for the son to drop out of college to support his mother and the other children. Or, for years one has prayed and planned to go to the foreign mission field, only to find that he cannot pass the strict medical and psychiatric examinations. Did God through his miraculous power or his direct intervention bring about these conditions that so drastically changed these plans? God might have and could have, but in the vast majority of cases he simply permits the laws of life to operate.

Let us return to the other question: Does God have a will for us when our whole world seems to collapse, whatever may be the cause of that collapse? Definitely yes; God has a plan or will for us in every circumstance of life.

A college senior was engaged to a young man who had graduated the year before. Their wedding date had been set. They had a deep conviction that they were within God's will in their plans. The young man suddenly took sick and died before his fiancée could get to him. Did God have a will for this young lady under such circumstances? I believe he did. It might be that he wanted her to remain single and give a life of devoted service to him and to her fellowman. But more probably his will was for her to marry another and with him build a Christian home. Several years later this is what she did.

In other words, whatever may be our circumstances in life, God has the resources to help us pick up the pieces and start building again. There is a very real sense in which his will is not only progressive but adaptable for every new experience.

The following statements help to sum up the matter: (1) We are not responsible for changes in the evident will of God in our lives that are beyond our control. (2) We should not be too ready, however, to shift the responsibility for changes in our plans from ourselves to others. (3) We must admit, in the light of our limitations, that we may be mistaken about what we think is the will of God. It is even possible that God may use circumstances of life to reveal his will more fully to us.

Preparatory to other decisions.—The last Missionary Day of each school year in our institution is a testimony service for those who have recently been appointed by our Foreign Mission Board. The wife of one of our students a few years ago told of the progressive revelation of the will of God regarding her lifework. While a college student she felt that it was God's will for her to teach in the public schools. She began her teaching career with a definite sense of divine purpose. After a couple of years, there came as a teacher to the same school a young preacher. She concluded, with some help from him, that God's will was for her to be a minister's wife. They married and later enrolled at Southwestern Seminary. In the warm evangelistic and missionary spirit of the campus she, along with her husband, felt that God wanted them as missionaries in Latin America. It is comparatively easy to see that each decision was another step toward the ultimate call to world mission service.

The frequently preparatory nature of decisions does not operate exclusively in the area of one's lifework. It is equally applicable to the whole area of right and wrong. Each wise, correct, or right decision prepares us for another. There seems to be a law of life operative in this whole area. Wrong decisions and right decisions tend to be cumulative. "Each vict'ry will help you some other to win," but each failure to do the right thing will tend to lead to another wrong decision.

Only as we follow the leadership of the Holy Spirit now can we be assured of his leadership in the future. Obedience to God's will in the daily decisions of life gives us added insight into his will. We shall see with increasing clarity that God has a will for every area of our lives—our relations within the family, the church, the school, the community. We shall also understand more and more clearly that God has a will for economic and political life, for the totality of our common life.

The life of Paul is an excellent illustration of the continuous, progressive nature of the will of God in one's life. When he met the resurrected Christ in that unusual experience on the Damascus road, he was told to go into the city and it would be revealed to him what he was to do. He had to be obedient to receive the revelation. At that time Ananias revealed, under the guidance of the Lord, the general outline of the purpose of God for his life. According to Paul, a portion of the statement of Ananias was as follows: "The God of our forefathers has destined and appointed you to come progressively to know His will—that is, to perceive, to recognize more strongly and clearly and to become better and more intimately acquainted with His will" (Acts 22:14, *Amplified New Testament*).

Let us review a few of the experiences of Paul that indicate a progressive knowledge of and co-operation with the will of God. He preached for a short period in Damascus. He then spent two or three years in Arabia. This was evidently a time of study, meditation, prayer, and preparation for his dynamic and fruitful ministry. After a brief visit to Damascus and to Jerusalem he "went into the regions of Syria and Cilicia" (cf. Gal. 1:11-21).

When Barnabas needed someone to help him in the great work at Antioch, he "went to Tarsus to look for Saul; and when he had found him, he brought him to Antioch" (Acts 11:25-26). It was while at Antioch that the Holy Spirit said, "Set apart for me Barnabas and Saul for the work to which I have called them. . . . After fasting and praying they laid their hands on them and sent them off" (13:2-3). Thus began the great missionary journeys of Paul.

On a later journey, Paul and his company were "forbidden by the Holy Spirit to speak the word in Asia." Again they "attempted to go into Bithynia, but the Spirit of Jesus did not allow them." Then notice what followed: "So, passing by Mysia, they went down to Troas." There Paul had his vision of a man of Macedonia saying, "Come over to Macedonia and help us" (Acts 16:6-10). In response to that voice the gospel was carried into Europe and the whole direction of Western civilization was affected.

This is enough to indicate that Paul's life was Spirit-led, that it was a life lived in progressive response to the will of God. If Paul had not been obedient to the resurrected Christ on the Damascus road, he would not and could not have had the vision at Troas.

But Paul, as he himself said to King Agrippa, "was not

disobedient to the heavenly vision" (Acts 26:19). You may say, "But I am not a Paul." No, but you and I are just as responsible as Paul for whatever insight we have regarding the will of God for our lives. Can we say, will we be able to say, "I was not disobedient to the heavenly vision"?

4

Choosing Your Lifework

It has been suggested that God's will applies to all, is always best, and is an expanding or a continuing experience for us. Another important characteristic of the will of God is that it is all-inclusive. It includes our lifework, our life's companion, and our daily decisions.

You have just one life to live, and it will be gone almost before you realize it. How tragic it will be if you make a mistake regarding your lifework. It may be tragic not only for you but also for your loved ones, your fellowman, and the cause of Christ! Surely, you will want to choose your lifework as intelligently and prayerfully as possible.

Perhaps you have already made this decision. If so, be sure to maintain an open mind for additional light. It is possible that God has something for you in the future that will be much richer and will make your life much more fruitful than anything you have dreamed about so far. You may have made your decision in the past but drifted away from it or become uncertain about it. Whatever your present situation, will you not covenant with the Lord that you will seek to know and to follow his will?

A plan for all.—The Bible plainly reveals that God had a plan for the life of Moses, Paul, and his other leaders. For example, Paul frequently referred to himself as an apostle of Jesus Christ "through the will of God" (e.g., 1 Cor. 1:1, KJV). He says he was set apart by the Lord before he was born (cf. Gal. 1:15). You may protest that you are not a Moses or a Paul. You may not even plan to enter a church-related vocation. Nevertheless, God has a plan for your life. It could not be otherwise of a God who created man in his own image and is so meticulous in his care of us that Jesus said, "Even the hairs of your head are all numbered" (Matt. 10:30). Surely such a God, who is our Heavenly Father, has a will concerning one of life's most important decisions!

This does not mean that God in some miraculous way will reveal his will or plan to you. He does this at times, but more frequently you will have to search, struggle, and pray before you have a definite sense of leading. This means, among other things, that God expects you to use every resource available in your search. This includes an objective analysis of your own personality, attitudes, and talents, along with an analysis of the demands and opportunities in various vocations. You can be sure that with rare exceptions God's will for your lifework will be in harmony with your capacities or talents. Consequently, you will get more joy and a deeper sense of fulfilment in doing work that is in harmony with God's will than in doing anything else.

God's unique call to some.—God has a plan for every life, but he seems to have a distinct or a unique call for some. There is a sense in which every child of God is in the ministry—he is to minister or serve. But there are some who, in a special way, are called or set apart by God to perform distinctive functions within the ministry of the church.

"God has appointed in the church first apostles, second prophets, third teachers" (1 Cor. 12:28). "His gifts were that some should be apostles, some prophets, some evangelists, some pastors and teachers" (Eph. 4:11). These were the ones who had places of special leadership in the life of the church. Paul addressed his Philippian letter "to all the saints in Christ Jesus who are at Philippi, with the bishops and deacons" (Phil. 1:1). He gave special qualifications for bishops and deacons (cf. 1 Tim. 3:1-13).

If we lose the conviction of a unique call for some we shall tend to lose the sense of God's plan or "call" for all. This is somewhat comparable to the relation of Sunday or the Lord's Day to the other days of the week. Every day should be a holy day for the child of God, a day dedicated or set apart unto God. There is one day, however, that is uniquely holy, the day on which Christ arose. This day belongs to God in a different way. And, if we lose the conviction regarding the unique holiness of this day, we shall tend, sooner or later, to lose the sense of the holiness of the less holy—the other days of the week.

God is interested in and has a plan for the lifework of every child of his, but it seems that he has an unusual interest in and concern for those who minister, more or less exclusively, in the things of the Spirit.

An Old Testament illustration may help to clarify this. It was just as much the will of God for David to be king over Israel as it was for Samuel to be his prophet. God, however, did not "call" David to be king; he did call Samuel to be his prophet or spokesman.

Whether or not God is calling or will call you into the pastoral ministry, the ministry of religious education, church music, or some other church-related vocation, your response to that call must be a personal decision. This call, if it comes, may be a clear-cut revelation from him, an outstanding, unforgettable experience. On the other hand, it may come as a gradual, deepening conviction that this is the will of God for your life. One call can be just as real and as abidingly meaningful as the other. Are you willing to respond to his call, in whatever way the call may come to you?

The New Testament reveals that a call to "the ministry" is basically a call to minister or serve; it is a call to an attitude of life more than to some exalted office.

It might help if I told you a little about my own call. It came in an unusually clear way when I was seventeen. It was a call "to preach"; but I had a conviction, even then, that I was never supposed to be the pastor of a church.

I could not understand why God would call me to preach, and yet would give me a feeling that I was not supposed to be a pastor. I struggled for years with the problem, trying to discover exactly what God wanted me to do. Over a period of time there developed a deepening conviction that teaching was his will for my life. I have never been ordained as a preacher.

As I look back and re-examine my experience, I can understand now that God had to call me to preach if he called me at all. It was the only call I knew anything about. He had to speak my language, otherwise I could not have responded. If I had known then what I know now about the New Testament ministry, I believe my call would have been a call to minister or serve rather than a call to preach. I believe that I am in the ministry just as much as my pastor.

God's universal calls.—While I believe strongly in the uniqueness of God's call to what is termed the Christian ministry, I also believe that many Christians tend to make too sharp a distinction between vocational religious workers and other Christians. Every child of God, in one sense, is supposed to be a "full-time" Christian worker. He may not be paid to render his Christian service, while the vocational worker is. Also, the latter may perform some distinctive functions, but the Christian farmer, business or professional man, or the Christian housewife should be a full-time Christian.

Many of God's expectations or "calls" are for all. In fact, his most basic "calls" or expectations are universal. For example, he expects every child of his to put his kingdom first. One's vocation or profession is to be dedicated to the promotion of that kingdom. If it cannot be, it had better be exchanged for one that can.

Every child of God is to be a witness for Christ—by word of mouth and by the quality of the life he lives. This he is to do not only within the walls of his church but also in his home, on the street, in the schoolroom, on the athletic field, in the shop or store—everywhere. In other words, Christ's "go ye therefore" and "ye shall be my witnesses" are addressed to all, just as much as his "follow me" and "come to me, all who labor and are heavy-laden." We must never forget that to follow him means to deny self and to take up a cross.

> Must Jesus bear the cross alone
> And all the world go free?
> No, there's a cross for ev'ry one,
> And there's a cross for me.

Another one of God's universal 'calls" is revealed in a statement by the apostle Paul: "God . . . chose to reveal his Son to me and through me, in order that I might proclaim him among the Gentiles" (Gal. 1:16, *The New English Bible*). We can be sure that God has chosen each of us to reveal his Son to us and through us to others. This is true, regardless of what our lifework may be. Our vocation is to be used as a means or a channel for the revelation of Christ.

Some time before he became a missionary, William Carey is reported to have said: "My business is to serve the Lord; I cobble shoes to pay expenses." Here is a great truth—our business, regardless of our present or future vocation, is to serve the Lord. But the statement also implies an error; i.e., the cobbling of shoes is not merely to pay expenses. It should be used as a means of service for God and man. The serious Christian will not be satisfied in his vocation unless he believes that in some way and to some degree his vocation, as such, can be used and is being used of God in achieving his purposes in the world.

Motivation.—As you examine or contemplate a decision regarding your lifework, it will be wise to consider possible motives. Guard against the material, which can become thoroughly pagan. The child of God is not to lay up or store up "treasures on earth" (Matt. 6:19); he "cannot serve God and mammon" (Matt. 6:24). "The love of money is the root of all evils" (1 Tim. 6:10). The desire for economic security should not become too prominent in your decision. Some consideration may properly be given to money and to security, but too much emphasis on the economic, and particularly on security, will tend to rob you of the adventuresome spirit, which is so essential in creative Christian living.

Another motive, very prevalent in the contemporary period, which must be guarded against is the desire for status or prestige. It is natural for all of us to desire some recognition, to want to attain some status within our circle of acquaintances. It will be unfortunate, however, for you to let this determine your lifework.

Other motives, some entirely worthy, may include a desire to please your loved ones or to serve your fellowman. Ultimately, however, the only adequate motive for the Christian is the desire to do the will of God. The wonderful thing is that if we discover and do his will, we shall find that it will be inclusive of every other worthy motive. For example, if we have a strong desire to serve our fellowman, to make the world a better place in which to live, we shall do this most fully as we follow the will of God for our lives.

Co-operation.—Whether or not we have been or will be called into a church-related vocation, we should co-operate with one another in the work of God in the world. There is no place in his service for a hierarchy of callings, for a feeling on the part of anyone that his calling is superior or inferior to that of someone else. In taking a picture at a youth camp, the boys who had volunteered for foreign mission service were placed in the front row; the ones who were planning on preaching in the states in the second row; others entering various forms of "religious service" in the third row; and the others behind them. This was entirely out of harmony with the spirit of the New Testament.

The highest "calling" for any child of God is to follow the will of God for his life. The Christian farmer with a sense of divine stewardship should be respected just as much as the foreign missionary; the Christian schoolteacher with a sense of divine mission should be respected just as much as the pastor with his sense of divine call. We may, and do, have distinctive functions to perform, but each can be used and blessed by him. So, be satisfied to perform your particular task, to fill your own peculiar place in his total program.

"We are labourers together with God" (1 Cor. 3:9, KJV). He will work with us if we will work with him. Let me give an illustration from my childhood. Before moving back to the farm, we lived for a number of years in a small town. We had an unusually large garden. Dad, who was a sturdy, strong man, could have tended that garden by himself. However, that did not fit in with his idea of rearing boys. He purchased a large garden plow, to which was attached a rope with a stick at the end of it. Then he placed my brother Red at one end of the stick and me at the other.

We pulled the plow as Dad guided it. I did not know then, but I am sure now that our father not only guided the plow but that he *pushed* more than both of us *pulled*. That is certainly true of our Heavenly Father. He depends on us to labor with him, but we can be sure that he pushes more than all of us pull.

5

Choosing Your Life's Companion

There is a "lover's leap" in Cameron Park, Waco, Texas. I do not know how many people have committed suicide by leaping from the ledge to the rocks below, but I do know that many young people "leap" recklessly into the choice of a life's companion and marriage. Some say that love is blind, but if the blind lead the blind they will frequently both fall into the ditch. If, when one chooses a companion for life his eyes are closed, they, in most cases, will be rather rudely opened soon after marriage.

Importance of the decision.—Many individuals have made the right decision concerning their lifework and yet wrecked their lives by an unwise choice of their companion. This decision frequently makes or breaks a man or a woman. The right companion will stimulate and enrich one's entire personality. It is hoped that you already have a deep resolve to choose your companion carefully and to seek God's will as definitely in this decision as in any other.

The choice of your companion is not only an important decision for you but also for the one who will be your companion—for both families, for society, for your church, and for the cause of Christ. In other words, there are many individuals and institutions that have a stake in the choice of your companion. While there is a sense in which this is a very personal matter, it is much more than that. If you are wise you will give some consideration to its impact on the others who in some way are involved in it.

It may help you, from the personal perspective, to recognize the seriousness of the decision if you will remember that you are not only choosing a companion but also the potential father or mother of your children. Another thing that points up the importance of the choice is its permanence. The decision is for life. God's original plan and his continuing ideal is that one man and one woman be joined together as husband and wife for life. That may be a long time. Ask yourself, "Is this the kind of individual I want to sit across the breakfast table from the rest of my life?" At least take time to "Stop! Look! Listen!"

Factors in the decision.—We cannot discuss all the factors that should be considered in the choice of a companion. Entire books have been written on this alone. The emphasis here is on the will of God. The Lord expects us to go about making this decision intelligently. We should keep our eyes, ears, and minds open and alert, and at the same time ask our Heavenly Father to lead us.

Consideration should be given to such things as age, native ability, and education—all of which ordinarily should be somewhere near your own. Also, proper consideration should be given to health—physical, mental, and emotional. The family background should be known. There is a sense in which you will marry the entire family; at least you can never get away from them. The general economic and cultural level should be known. All of the preceding matters should be given consideration, but possibly no one of them should be the determining factor.

Congeniality of interests and ideals could be spelled out in considerable detail. Let me simply suggest that as a child of God you will want to look for basic character. There are few things more important in the choice of a life's companion than this. Set your standards high. Do not be too quick to adjust them, but at the same time, do not

expect perfection. After all, you are not perfect! The best
assurance of marrying someone who measures up reason-
ably well to your ideals is to measure up to them yourself.

God's will concerning this decision.—While you are
studying possible mates, do not forget to pray. Prayer, in
this as well as in every other area of our lives, should not
be something that is tacked on or added after we have
done everything else. The spirit of prayer should permeate
all that we do. Start praying and seeking the leadership of
the Lord before you "fall in love." After you are, or think
you are, in love, you can persuade yourself that almost
anything is the will of God.

The consideration of one major factor in the choice of
a life's companion has been delayed until now. A Christian
should choose a Christian. It is assumed that you want a
Christian home. You cannot have such a home without a
Christian companion. Being a Christian cannot necessarily
be equated with church membership. You cannot have a
real Christian home without a real Christian as a companion. This is one factor that should be determinative in
the choice of a companion by a Christian youth.

The Bible speaks rather specifically regarding this matter. Paul said it was all right for a widow to marry "whom
she wishes, only in the Lord" (1 Cor. 7:39)—one who is in
the Lord or a Christian. If Paul would say that for a widow,
would he not say the same thing to Christian young people? Paul in another place states a general principle, which
is clearly applicable to marriage. He says, "Do not be mismated with unbelievers" (2 Cor. 6:14), or "Be ye not unequally yoked together with unbelievers" (KJV). For one
to marry a non-Christian is to be "mismated" or "unequally
yoked." Such a home cannot fulfil the high purpose of God.
It is only the real Christian home that can be used by God
to promote his kingdom in the world.

It is wise for a Christian youth to choose a companion of his or her own religious faith. At least, religious differences should be worked out before marriage. Surely, it is not God's will for a family to be divided regarding so important a matter. It is particularly unwise for a Protestant young person to choose as a companion one who belongs to the Roman Catholic Church. The differences are too great. Too much would have to be surrendered by the Protestant. If you are considering such a marriage, talk with your pastor or some other counselor.

Questions related to the decision.—What about "the one and only"? It has been suggested that one's companion be within the will of God. Does this mean that there is only one? If this is true, what should one do if that one refuses to co-operate with the will of God? Should he or she remain single, or if he chooses another can he expect any real happiness and satisfaction?

When a husband and wife have a deep conviction that they have been led together by the Lord, there is a depth of happiness and satisfaction that they would never have known otherwise. God's will, however, is no more automatically done in this area than in any other area of our lives. If what you consider his will does not work out, he does not expect you to pine away the rest of your life. You can still find real happiness and have a sense of being within the will of God.

Another question that young people occasionally ask is: "Do you think one can fall in love at first sight?" Many students of the family consider this impossible. It may be possible but not probable. There is one thing, however, that I am quite sure about: it will not hurt to take a second look.

Take time to read Genesis 24, which contains a story that is old in its customs but abidingly relevant in its central concepts. Notice particularly the following: The servant was not to take a wife for Isaac among the Canaanites, who did not worship the true God (v. 3); the assurance of Abraham that God would send his angel before his servant (v. 7); the servant asked God to prosper his journey (vv. 12-14); when the servant's prayer was answered he bowed his head and worshiped the Lord (vv. 26-27). The family of Rebekah said, "The thing comes from the Lord' (v. 50); Rebekah, attractive and a virgin (v. 16), with a venturesome faith consented to go with the servant of Abraham (v. 58); she became the wife of Isaac "and he loved her" (v. 67).

A personal testimony.—I have not been preaching something to you that I did not practice. Let me share with you something of my experience.

While in high school, I began to realize that my companion was a part of God's plan and will for my life. Before I began dating regularly or seriously I prayed almost daily that God would lead me to the one he had for me.

During college days there was a growing conviction that a certain classmate was the one he wanted me to have as my life's companion. This conviction was quite strong before I ever had a date with her. We had classes together and had worked together in religious organizations on the campus and in our church life and activities. I had talked informally with her many times. I knew her quite well even before our first date.

The conviction that she was *the* one deepened as we dated for some months. During this time we shared freely our motives, ambitions, purposes, and dreams. We became acquainted with each other's families.

The day we became engaged is one we cherish very much. Its memory is very sacred. I have shared what happened on that day only a few times. Our date that Sunday afternoon was under the maple trees on the campus of

Carson-Newman College. I had previously decided that I was going to propose to her that day. Before I left my room in Davis Hall to have that date I got down on my knees and asked our Heavenly Father that his will might be done. After I had asked her and she had said yes, I learned that she likewise had knelt by her bed before our date and had asked that God would lead in our lives.

I wish you could know how much this has meant to us. We have walked together more years than you have lived. There have been sorrows as well as joys, rough places as well as smooth, but through it all there has been the deep consciousness that we were led together of the Lord. This has been our joy, our peace, our security in one another. My hope and prayer for you is that you may have a comparable experience.

6

Making Daily Decisions

Many of the seemingly minor decisions often help to set the direction of our lives. Frequently they influence, or determine ahead of time, the major decisions. So, in a very real sense, every decision is potentially a major one.

Related to lifework.—Decisions preceding, as well as succeeding, the choice of your lifework may be quite important. Among these is the question of college. If college is within the purpose of God for your life, then what college—denominational or state? Once in college, you must decide how much emphasis to give to extracurricular activities, what organizations to join, what to major in, how to spend your summers, and so on. Any one of such decisions could set the direction of your life.

Adequate preparation is as much within the will of God as your lifework itself. God wants us to be our best and to do our best. We should not be satisfied with anything less than the best possible preparation for our God-chosen vocation. Many individuals with unusual native ability, and even with unquestioned Christian devotion, fail to measure up to God's potential for them because they fail to prepare adequately. The foundation on which they seek to build is insufficient. They soon reach the peak of their achievement and level off or decline prematurely.

It may not take much of a foundation to build a chicken house, but it takes a deep and solid one to build a temple of God or a skyscraper that reaches up toward heaven.

Which do you want your life to be? Will you pay the necessary price in discipline, energy, time, and money to prepare thoroughly?

Every child of God should recognize that God wants him to work diligently at his task. The hardest working individuals on the campus or in the business community should be those who sense a divine purpose working in and through them.

Still another decision is "where" one works. God may want you as a business or professional person or as a government employee to go to some needy area in the homeland or even in some foreign country. Thus, you could just as truly become an ambassador for Christ as the so-called missionary.

All of us can be sure that God is not only concerned about our lifework but he is also concerned about how Christian we are in our daily tasks. We should seek his guidance here just as definitely as we did in choosing our lifework. We should seek as best we can to apply the Christian spirit and Christian principles to our day-by-day activities. It is possible for us to choose our vocation in harmony with the will of God and yet be outside of his will in the way we participate in that vocation.

Young women face some distinctive problems. While it is evidently God's will for most of them to marry and have a family, this seemingly is not true for all. If the young woman marries should she, and can she, successfully have a career outside of the home and still be a good wife and mother? If she definitely plans to be a housewife, should she prepare for a career? The answer to these and related questions should largely be personal decisions.

The Christian young woman should seek, however, at all times to know the will of God. If it is his will for her to remain single, she can be assured that she can have a meaningful life of service as she fulfils God's purpose for her life. If she has a strong desire for a career, she should seriously search her own soul to see if she would be willing to put her family first, which evidently is the plan and purpose of God. She should also examine her motives regarding a career. She will doubtless conclude that it will be wise for her to prepare for a career as well as for a homemaker, even though she anticipates giving herself exclusively to marriage and her home. She knows that she can never know when she may need the skills of a career.

It should be added that young men should prepare far more adequately than most of them do for their role as husbands and fathers. It is also possible that God, at least in some cases, would want a young man to remain single. There have been some wonderful servants of the Lord who, under divine impulse, have never married.

Relating to life's companion.—Since God is concerned about the quality of life we live, you can be sure that he is concerned about and has a will regarding your dating habits. Most students of the family agree that there are some rather common unwise dating practices, such as dating too young, going steady prematurely, and petting too freely and promiscuously which frequently leads to premarital sex relations. It is not our purpose here to discuss these matters but simply to say that God has a will regarding such things. These practices tend to create many problems, one of the most serious of which is an unwise choice of a companion and marriage at too early an age.

The latter implies that God may have a purpose regarding the timing of this major decision and of the marriage itself. I am not trying to dictate to you where, when, or whom you marry. But I am suggesting that these may all be tied into one bundle in the will of God and, as a Christian youth, you should seek to know and do his will.

You may be already married. If so, you know, of course, that God has a will for your relations together in the home. It is possible for a couple to have a deep conviction that they have been led together by the Lord and yet fail in their marriage because they do not follow God's leadership in their daily decisions.

Concerning right or wrong.—Some of the most perplexing decisions for some young Christians are in the area of right or wrong. We cannot discuss the specific problems. This has been done, to some degree, in my book *Right or Wrong?* (published by Broadman Press in 1955). Here, I shall simply ask some questions and make a few suggestions.

First, where is the child of God supposed to get his standards of right and wrong? Is the right to be determined for him by what others say or do, or by what God wills? Is he to conform to the culture that surrounds him, to the standards of his particular crowd, or is he to conform to the spirit and teachings of Christ?

God's will should be supreme for us in our daily decisions, and his will is grounded in and is an expression of his basic nature. His nature, as well as his will, was revealed by Jesus who "bears the very stamp" of the nature of God (cf. Heb. 1:3). If we want to follow the will of God for our lives, let us walk the paths that Jesus walked. It will be difficult to walk that high road, but an honest attempt to do so will pay rich dividends.

Paul's admonition to the Ephesians is applicable to you and to me. He says, "Look carefully . . . how you walk, not as unwise men but as wise." He also admonishes them not to be foolish but to "understand what the will of the Lord is" (5:15,17). It is wise to walk in the way of the Lord. It is foolish not to seek to know and to do his will regarding our daily decisions.

Take the long look. What do you want your life to be twenty to twenty-five years from now? Your decisions today are determining, to a considerable degree, whether or not your dreams will become realities. The best assurance that your dreams will come true is to live from day to day within the will of God.

Concerning the positive quality of life.—Do not belittle or play down the so-called negatives or the thou-shalt-nots. Many times a decision regarding one of these negatives may be the most important immediate decision for a particular young person at a particular time. However, the final and highest expression of the Christian life is positive. We need to recognize this in our daily decisions. We may not partcipate in any of the so-called questionable activities; still we may not be good Christians. Good Christians will not do those things that would hurt them personally, would handicap the cause of Christ, or would be a stumbling block to others. Yet, the supreme test of the Christian life is a positive one.

How much of the spirit of Christ do we have in our lives? How much of his way of life do others see in us—our loved ones, our friends, our roommate, our teammate, the one who works by our side? How clearly do they see the resurrected Christ revealed in our lives on Monday through Saturday as well as on Sunday? Do they see his spirit expressed in and through us in our attitudes toward and our relations to young and old, to the physically and mentally handicapped, the economically underprivileged, the moral outcasts, and those of other classes and races? How much they see of Christ revealed through us in the classroom, in the dorm, at home, and everywhere else will be determined by how much we let him live in us.

Toward the close of his life, Jesus said to the inner circle of his disciples, "You did not choose me, but I chose you

and appointed you that you should go and bear fruit"
(John 15:16). Notice the purpose of the choosing or the
appointment. This is his over-all purpose in your life and
mine. And we shall be fruitful to the degree that we maintain a vital relation to Christ. He is the vine, we are the
branches. The lifeblood of the vine flowing through the
branches is the source of their fruit bearing (cf. John
15:4-5).

Concerning the ultimate goal of our lives.—God's will
is so broad, so deep, so high, so inclusive that none of us
will ever fully attain it. To do so would mean perfection.
The impossibility of fully attaining his will should not discourage us, but it should constantly challenge us.

God's ultimate ideal or will for us is our holiness or
sanctification (cf. 1 Thess. 4:3). We were justified in his
sight in the initial experience when we became children of
God. There is a sense in which we were sanctified or set
apart unto God in that experience, but there is also a very
real sense in which our sanctification is a lifetime process.
We have been saved (justified) but we are also in the
process of being saved (sanctified). The latter has both its
negative and positive aspects.

Sanctification involves separation from the evils of the
world to a dedication to God. Peter expressed something of
this twofold emphasis when he said, "As obedient children,
do not be conformed to the passions of your former ignor-
ance, but as he who called you is holy, be holy yourselves
in all your conduct; since it is written, 'You shall be holy,
for I am holy'" (1 Peter 1:14-16; cf. Lev. 19:2).

There is a sense in which God's will for our lives reaches
beyond this life. This is implied in what has been said regarding holiness or santification—it is never fully attained
in this life. The ultimate goal of the Christian's life, which
is a glorious one, is that he shall awake at the end of life's

journey in the likeness of the resurrected Christ. We also hope and pray that at that time we shall hear, "Well done." If we can have his approval, that will be enough reward for any price we may have paid to do his will.

In closing this chapter and this section of our study, let us meditate upon the following prayer of Paul. Examine it phrase by phrase:

I have never ceased praying for you and asking God to fill you, through full wisdom and spiritual insight, with a clear knowledge of His will, so that you may lead lives worthy of the Lord to His full satisfaction, by perennially bearing fruit in every good enterprise and by a steady growth in fuller knowledge of God; then you will be perfectly empowered by His glorious might for every sort of joyous endurance and forbearance (Col. 1:9-11, Williams).

Part II: How Can We Know God's Will?

7

Use Personal Resources

Perhaps you have already asked yourself, How can I know the will of God? Or, can I know the will of God?

The answer to the latter question depends on what is meant by "the will of God" and by the word "know." Are the terms used in a relative or in an absolute or perfect sense? If in the relative, the answer would be yes; if in the absolute, the answer would have to be no.

Man can know the will of God but never fully or perfectly. God's will is too big, too broad, and too deep for the most mature of us ever to understand it completely. However, we are not left adrift in the world without any sense of divine direction. The experiences of many children of God, perhaps including you, prove that we can have enough insight into the will of God to take the next necessary step. We can know what we need to know at a particular point in time. We can look forward to increasingly rich experiences as we seek to follow God's will for our lives.

On the other hand, as has been true with me, you may find it difficult at times to know the will of God. This is one reason why we should consider every possible resource that is available to us in our search for his will. Let's consider a number of approaches we can make in our search. We should consider all of them as one package or bundle. They belong together. In some ways they supplement each other. We cannot wisely eliminate any one of them. To varying degrees, all of them are necessary if we are to know the will of God. They are all good gifts from God and should be utilized in our search for his guidance.

Before we discuss the first of these "good gifts from God," permit me to state an assumption, make a statement, and ask a question. The assumption: That you are active in the work of your church—its teaching and training program, its worship services, its evangelistic and missionary outreach. The statement: The best assurance of knowing the will of God in the future is to be within his will now. The question: Is there any doubt in your mind about being within the will of God now?

The Bible plainly reveals that man was created in the image of God. When man sinned, that image was marred or defaced but not totally destroyed. This image is restored, in a sense, when man becomes a new creation through union with Christ, who is the exact image of the Father. However, the restoration will not be complete until the end of life's journey, when we shall awake in Christ's likeness.

The incompleteness of the restoration explains the continuing hunger of the child of God for a deeper and more meaningful communication with the Heavenly Father. This inner hunger often is more pronounced in the lives of God's most mature children. The more we know about the nature and will of God, the more clearly we see how much there is still to know.

This deepening desire to know is closely related to and dependent upon a strong desire to be obedient to his will. God expects us to use whatever capacities we have in our search for his will. He seldom reveals his will to us in a miraculous way. We can be sure, however, that he will respond as we seek to know.

Our rational nature.—God has given to us our rational nature. He expects us to use it. Some plain common sense,

which is not too common, will be a great asset in our search
for the purposes of God.

Let us apply the common sense test to one or two specific
matters. God evidently does not want a young man who has
flunked his science courses and does not have the grades to
be admitted to a medical school to go as a medical
missionary. Similarly, common sense would suggest that it
would be unwise for a woman of forty to marry a man of
twenty. These are extreme examples, but the proper use of
the common sense that God has given you will help you in
practically every decision relating to your lifework or your
life's companion. When making these major decisions, do
not let your mind take a vacation.

The ability to think straight or to use common sense will
also help, over and over again, in the daily decisions of life.
When considering the rightness or wrongness of some particular activity, think about the potential consequences. Observe in others the results of such activities. For example,
if you are debating whether to accept or decline the cock-
tail when it is offered, observe what drinking has done for
others—some of your friends or loved ones. Study the number of crimes committed by people who have been drinking. Study reports from the public safety commission, show-
ing the number of fatal accidents that are caused by drinking drivers. Think of the number of alcoholics in the United
States—men and women who have become slaves of alcohol. The estimates vary but there are at least five million,
and the number is constantly increasing. If you want to see
what drink really does, visit your city or county jail on a
Saturday night or on a holiday weekend.

One of the most pathetic alcoholics I know is a brilliant,
scholarly man of about forty-five. He had risen to the top
in his profession but recently was relieved of all his responsibilities for a year. If he does not rid himself of this prob-

lem in that time he is through—a useful and brilliant career ended.

You may be saying, "All of this does not apply to me; I can go ahead and drink and keep it under control." Can you? How do you know you can? Actually, no one can know for sure whether or not he will have a weakness for drink. When one takes that first drink he may take the first step toward slavery to alcohol.

Common sense would dictate that one should never take the first drink. Even if one could be entirely sure that he would never become an alcoholic, there are still many valid arguments against drinking.

Common sense also would dictate the same position regarding smoking. I do not need a special revelation from God to tell me whether or not to smoke. The American Cancer Society and other groups have given me the answer.

Through intelligent observation and the application of common sense, you can find the help you need for many other problems you face. Some of these problems, such as cheating, gambling, movies, Sunday observance, dancing, and petting, along with drinking and smoking, are discussed in my book *Right or Wrong?*

Our conscience.—This is not the place for a technical discussion of the nature of conscience. Two or three statements may be helpful, however, about what we do and do not mean by the use of the term "conscience." We do not mean that man has some innate capacity that will unerringly guide him in the right way. God has placed within man a sense of oughtness, an inborn conviction that there is such a thing as right and wrong. This is a part of man's equipment for knowing the will of God. It makes a man a morally responsible person.

In contrast to this innate sense of oughtness, the content of one's conscience, what he considers to be right or wrong, is not inborn. It depends largely on his total moral experience—what he has been taught in the home and the church, the attitudes of friends and loved ones, and personal experiences.

While all of us will agree that there is such a thing as right or wrong, we will frequently differ regarding the things or activities we consider right or wrong. This implies that one can follow what he considers his conscience and be wrong. Thus, his conscience needs to be educated, it needs to be made more sensitive. Conscience is not the voice of God, although it may be "the ear of the soul." The ear, however, needs to be trained.

Does this mean that we cannot trust and, hence, we should not follow our conscience? As previously suggested, our conscience will not always be right. However, we should always do what it says is right. There is a difference between the inerrancy of conscience and its authority. It errs or makes mistakes at times but it should be obeyed. The best assurance of a more sensitive conscience later is to be responsive to the one we now have. In other words, deliberate wrongdoing or going contrary to our conscience would affect adversely our moral judgment. This means that it is both wrong and unwise to do what our conscience tells us is wrong for us to do.

We have a twofold responsibility to our conscience—to obey it and to educate it. If we keep these two responsibilities in proper perspective, we shall find that what we call our conscience can and will aid us considerably in our search for the will of God.

Our limitations.—It has been suggested that man's personal resources are limited. It has been implied that if we could think straight we would see the wisdom of doing the will of God. But, unfortunately, it is impossible for us to think entirely straight. Sin has affected our total personality, including our rational nature. Our inability to think consistently straight helps to explain the undependability of our conscience. It is true that we are limited; nevertheless, God expects us to use what we have. We should admit the limitations of our natural resources and then recognize our need for help as we seek to know and to do the will of God. This inability to trust completely our own resources may have been the background for a statement by W. O. Carver that helped me a great deal in a time of major decision. I was in his home adjacent to the campus of Southern Baptist Theological Seminary, where he taught for many years. I had not gone to seek his advice, but he gave it anyway:

"When you have considered a matter from every conceivable viewpoint, if your mind tells you one thing and your heart tells you something else, you had better follow your heart." He was saying, if I interpreted him correctly, that one had better follow the inner impression that comes from the leadership of the Holy Spirit. On that occasion I followed my heart rather than my head, and through the years I have been grateful that God used Dr. Carver to drop that thought or guideline into my life.

Do not conclude from this illustration that the head and the heart always conflict. Many times they are in perfect harmony or speak the same language. After all, it will be the part of wisdom to have the head check the heart. Only the individual who can and will think objectively can be trusted to follow his inner impressions.

8

Seek Counsel of Others

One source of help that is rather readily available to all of us in our search for the will of God is the counsel or the advice of others—friends, parents, teachers, and church leaders and workers. You will find these to be "good gifts from God," gifts that are precious, that should be respected and used properly and wisely. You may take the initiative and go to one or more of them for counsel. On the other hand, they, at times, may take the initiative in giving advice to you. Their counsel may be given to you personally or in and through a group. It is also possible that some of the best advice you will ever receive will be given incidentally and unconsciously.

Counseling that is sought.—You may have already felt the need for some help outside of yourself. You turned to your parents, to a friend, a teacher, your pastor, or someone else for assistance. You shared with them your problem or problems. You should not hesitate to do this when there is a real need in your life, but guard against becoming too dependent on others. A part of the maturing process is increasing capacity, with the Lord's help, to make our own decisions, to stand on our own feet. Do not become "a counselor addict." There are those who seek the counsel of almost everyone who is available. They seem to *enjoy* sharing their problems with others, but they do very little to solve them. In many cases they know what they ought to do, but seem to lack the will power or the strength of character to do it. Some of them evidently enjoy their continuing state of indecision.

Let me repeat, however, do not hesitate to seek help if you find that you need it. This should be done even in utilizing and interpreting the abundant spiritual resources that God has made available to all of his children. Frequently someone more mature can be of great assistance to you in interpreting the leadership of the Lord in your life.

When you find it advisable to counsel with someone, select carefully the one to whom you go. He or she should be a person who will understand you, one whom you respect, who will be objective, can be trusted, has a mature Christian perspective, and has the skill to be helpful. Do not expect to receive from that individual a complete answer to your problem, neatly wrapped up in a package. There is no cut and dried or standard answer to any problem. You will discover that the wise counselor will usually refuse to tell you exactly what you ought to do. He will help you think through your problem, and examine with you the different facets of it, thus giving a basis on which you can determine for yourself what is best.

This indirect approach will be much better for you than for someone to try to hand out to you a ready-made solution for your problem. The making of your own decisions is a part of the maturing process. It is your right as a human being, and particularly as a Christian, but it is also your responsibility—a responsibility that cannot be escaped and may at times rest very heavily on young shoulders. Even if, at your insistence, the counselor gives you his opinion, he will likely suggest that you should do what you personally consider to be the will of God for your life.

Counseling that is given.—There will be occasions when advice will be given voluntarily. You may not seek it and may not have a felt need for it. Such advice may come from friends, teachers, church leaders, but most frequently it will come from your parents. They live with you. They have a better opportunity than others to know you and your needs. Usually they feel freer than others to speak to you. You can be sure that in the vast majority of cases they are more interested in you and your welfare than anyone else. They have more at stake in your life. In a very real sense, you are a part of them. They would like to save you from some of the mistakes they made. They have traveled the route before. They know some of the dangers along the way. Life has been a teacher to them. They would like to pass on to you some of the lessons they have learned. And, the more thoroughly Christian they are, the deeper is their concern for you and the stronger is their desire that you walk in the way that God would have you go.

Young people need to be careful about their reactions to their parents' counsel. Some may tend to resent or ignore it. I hope this is not true of you. I hope that you have already passed through the stage, which seems to be inevitable, when young people tend more or less to rebel against their parents. This rebellion seems to be a part of "the conflict of the generations." You will come to the place, if you are not there now, when you will consider your parents among the wisest of people.

Parents are not perfect. All of us make mistakes, but I can assure you that most of the mistakes that we make as parents are honest mistakes. You are ours; we want the best for you. You are to be our representative in the world. This means, among other things, that the counsel your parents give you comes, in the vast majority of cases, from a concerned heart. This, in turn, means that you should give serious consideration to their advice. If you disagree and do not follow their advice, you should at least be courteous and understanding. Do not forget that you are human as well as they. You may discover later that you were wrong and they were right, while on the other hand, they may discover later that they were wrong and you were right. Regardless, it will be helpful for you to remind yourself that some day you may stand where they now stand.

If I were writing primarily for parents the approach and emphasis in this section would be considerably different. I would suggest that parents help their sons and daughters grow toward maturity. Build into their lives basic Christian principles and ideals that will enable them to make their decisions wisely. Increasingly shift to them the responsibility for making decisions and recognize that the maturing Christian son or daughter owes supreme allegiance to the will of God.

God's will must be individually interpreted. This means, among other things, that you as a Christian young person may find it necessary at times, in response to the will of God, to go contrary to parental advice. This does not nullify at all what has been said about your respect for your parents and your serious consideration of their counsel.

Group counseling.—In addition to face-to-face counseling, there are frequent opportunities for counseling in groups. Possibly you already have discovered that such counseling can be very helpful as you seek to know the will of God concerning your life. Through group discussions you may receive significant help in solving a problem that you would not care to discuss personally with others. This may be true regarding some of the most difficult and delicate decisions you will make.

In this section we shall restrict our consideration to the more or less formal group discussions, which are in contrast to the informal groups that are largely unconscious of any counseling purpose. The latter will be briefly discussed in the next section.

Group counseling can be done at school, at church, or at camp. It may be the feature of a Sunday evening fellowship or a youth retreat, conducted as a panel or group discussion, or a question and answer session. It may be led by young people, older people, or even by "experts." It may be called a youth conference, open forum, or seminar. It may concentrate on one subject, such as lifework, love and marriage, some particular problem in the area of "right and wrong," or on some social, philosophical, or theological problem. On the other hand, the discussion may be general, dealing with anything the participants want to consider.

Regardless of the type of group and the method used, the effectiveness of group discussions will depend largely upon the background and the skill of the leader and the alertness and responsiveness of the participants.

Unconscious counseling.—Some of the best help you will ever receive as you seek the will of God will come from individuals and groups when there is no conscious attempt to advise you. It may be a conversation with a friend or with a group of friends at your church or on the campus. Or, it may be the casual contacts and conversations with loved ones in the home or on the highway. Sometimes guidance comes to us simply through the general impact that is made. Association with real Christian people tends to make us more sensitive to the touch of God on our lives. There will also be times when a chance remark is lodged in our minds that will be quite helpful to us. My own life has been tremendously influenced by about a half-dozen statements casually made by others without any evident purpose to counsel or influence me.

You may understand better what I am attempting to say if I give you a personal illustration. My brother, older than I and a young businessman, dropped by Carson-Newman College to visit me when I was a freshman. He and I were walking from the business district of the small town toward the campus. I do not remember what we were discussing, but I have never gotten away from the impact of one statement he made that day. I could go to the spot on the sidewalk on Russell Street where he made it. The statement was, "Remember, Tom, folks will respect a fellow who stands for something." That statement has come to me over and over again when I have had to decide whether or not a certain thing was right or wrong for me to do.

Watch for help that comes from these unconscious sources. If you will keep alert you will discover attitudes and ideas, as well as statements, that may be tremendously helpful to you. As suggested, you may pick these things up from loved ones or friends. You may also receive some real guidance in the Sunday school class, the youth program, or the regular worship services of your church. The last of these—worship—helps in a marvelous way to open our minds and hearts to the leadership of the Lord.

Printed materials.—This is an additional source of help to which we could justifiably devote a chapter or even a book. Through the printed page, individuals you have never met can speak to you. This may be true of pamphlets, magazine articles, Sunday school lessons, youth programs, study course books, guidance books, biographies, and others. Some of the help will be direct, some indirect. What is available in your school and church libraries? Have you formed the habit of reading good literature? Some of you will be helped as much by what you read as in any other way. This is an untapped source of help for many Christian young people.

Counseling and personal responsibility.—Regardless of how much help you may receive from others, either through personal or group counseling, the final decision regarding the will of God in your life must be your own decision. While we were children our parents had to make many decisions for us. One part of the maturing process, however, is the right and the responsibility to make our own decisions.

In seeking the will of God for your life, there may be rare occasions when you feel compelled to go contrary to all the advice that has been given. If such a situation arises, be very cautious. Be sure that you are following the leadership of the Lord—not your own personal desires. Recognize the possibility that you may be wrong. Remember that one evidence of growing maturity is the consideration one gives to the counsel of more mature people. The immature tends to assert prematurely his right to make his own decisions without a comparable sense of responsibility for these decisions.

9

Study the Bible

Our Heavenly Father is impartial in the distribution of his best gifts. One of these best gifts to us is the Bible. Unfortunately, it is largely an unknown book, even for many of God's children. It is unknown to some because it is unopened. We cannot know the Bible; hence we cannot have the guidance that it would give to us unless we will take the time to read, study, and prayerfully meditate upon it. Some Christians may contend that they do not understand it when they read it. They prefer to accept what someone else says it means. One of the marvels of the Bible, however, is the fact that although the scholar cannot in a lifetime of study exhaust its depth and meaning, any honest searching Christian heart can understand its basic truths.

Its specific teachings.—There are many places where the Bible speaks a plain word on a particular subject or problem. Surely all of us will agree that when it does, such a statement is an expression of the will of God. There are so many of these statements that we cannot take the time or space even to list them.

The Ten Commandments provide a good illustration of the Bible's specific teachings. In a sense, they summarize the basic moral laws of the Old Testament. They pointedly say that the children of God shall have no other gods, nor make any graven image, nor take God's name in vain. The sabbath day should be kept holy and parents should be honored. It is also clearly stated that it is wrong or contrary to God's will for one to kill, to commit adultery, to steal, to bear false witness, or to covet.

Some of these Commandments can be variously interpreted, but this does not affect their validity as a source for the will of God in the areas covered. It should be remembered that these words have back of them the authority of the sovereign God of the universe. He speaks through them to every age. When one kills, commits adultery, steals, bears false witness, or covets, he breaks a commandment of God, and one cannot break a basic law of God without sooner or later paying the penalty for the violation.

There is an abundance of other specific teachings on many subjects in both the Old and New Testaments. Let us sum up by saying that when we properly read and interpret these teachings we shall find in them an expression of the will of God for our lives.

Possibly a word or two of caution should be sounded. While we should be obedient to what we interpret to be the voice of God to us through the Scriptures, let us not become too dogmatic about our own particular interpretation. Many passages can be interpreted in various ways. We have the right and the responsibility to read, interpret, and apply the Scriptures for ourselves, but we should give and defend the same right for others.

We should also be careful that we do not attempt to make the Bible a rule book with an authoritative, cut and dried answer for every question. We should recognize that we cannot find a chapter and verse solution for every problem. It would not be best for us if it were that kind of a book. We would not have the maturing process of struggling, through careful Bible study and prayer, to know the will of God in our lives. We would be robbed of some of the richest blessings that can come to us as children of God.

Also, if our Bible were a rule book this would tend to formalize or solidify the will of God. But God's will is not static; it is dynamic and should be such in our lives. We will find as we walk in his will that it will constantly expand for us. This will even be true of our insights into the expressions of his will in the Bible. It may be wise, however, to suggest again that the only assurance of a deepened insight into the Scriptures is present obedience to the voice of God as he speaks to us through those Scriptures.

Its general principles.—We have suggested that we can be helped by the proper reading, interpreting, and application of the specific teachings of the Scriptures. Many of us will receive, however, as much if not more help in our search for the will of God from a knowledge of the basic concepts or general principles of the Bible. This help may not be as direct but it will frequently be broader in its application. Furthermore, the ideas and ideals inherent in these principles will provide tone and direction for our lives. They will not only help us to know the will of God, they also will deepen our desire to walk in his will. They will even provide a basis for the proper interpretation of the specific teachings of the Bible.

Many of these basic concepts, such as holiness, righteousness, love, justice, mercy, impartiality, and self-denial, are found throughout the Bible. However, these and other general principles are particularly prominent in the life and teachings of Jesus. He restricted himself in his teachings, in the main, to the enunciation of general principles or ideals. That is one reason for the abiding relevance of his teachings.

Let us refer to just one incident in the life of Jesus. A lawyer, representing the Pharisees, asked him, "Teacher, which is the great commandment in the law?" Jesus, quoting two commandments from the Old Testament (Deut.

6:5; Lev. 19:18), replied: "You shall love the Lord your God with all your heart, and with all your soul, and with all your mind. This is the great and first commandment. And a second is like it, You shall love your neighbor as yourself." There is then added, "On these two commandments depend all the law and the prophets" (Matt. 22:34-40). When we understand this to mean that we are to love God with our total personalities and that our "neighbor" includes anyone of any class or race who needs our love, then we see that here in these two commandments there is enough to challenge us to the end of life's journey. Here are ideals that will provide guidelines for us in times of decision.

Its indirect help.—The Bible will not only help us know the will of God through its specific teachings and its general principles but also by its general effect on us as we read it. Its spirit tends to grip and permeate our lives. Our minds become enlightened, our emotions stirred, and our wills moved to respond to the leadership of the Holy Spirit. This means that we shall not only understand more clearly the will of God, but that we shall also have a deepening desire to do his will.

It should be unnecessary to say that these blessings will come only to those who read and study the Bible meditatively and prayerfully. It is particularly important to read the Gospels—the biographies of Jesus. He fully revealed the Father, and hence he fully revealed the way in which the Father would have us walk. Let us saturate our very souls in the life and teachings of Jesus and let his spirit grip our lives.

Its proper study.—We should have some regular habits of Bible reading and study. This should include more than reading to check a record or to prepare a Sunday school lesson or an assignment in a Bible course in college. These are important, but we need to do some reading strictly for devotional purposes. If we are to be blessed by our reading and study, we must approach the Bible with an open mind and a sincerely searching heart.

If you want the maximum benefit from studying the Bible, do not read in a hurry. There will be times when a particular verse grips you. Stop and meditate upon it. Let the truth it contains permeate and become an abiding part of your life.

Some years ago, traveling by train to Ridgecrest, North Carolina, I was about as despondent and blue as I ever get. In connection with some writing I was doing, I was reading the Bible. Suddenly one verse almost jumped out of the page: "When I fall, I shall arise; when I sit in darkness, the Lord shall be a light unto me" (Micah 7:8, KJV). I did not remember ever having read the verse, and had never heard a preacher or teacher quote or refer to it in a message. I read it and reread it. I closed my Bible and let its great truth soak into my very soul. It was the particular message I needed. God used it to bless my life then and many times since.

Its authority.—Most Christians agree that the source of authority for man is outside of man rather than within him, that there is an absolute or an eternal source of authority. This absolute source is the will of God, and since the will of God is in harmony with and an expression of the nature of God, the ultimate source of authority for man is in God himself.

How is the Bible and its authority related to the preceding? The Bible is our best tangible and objective (in contrast to subjective) source for a knowledge of the nature and will of God. This is the basis for its authority. It possesses no authority apart from God. Its authority is grounded in God. There is a sense in which the Bible's au-

thority does not reside within itself. In other words, its
authority is not based primarily on the words of the printed
page but on the revelation of God that gave birth to the
words. In the final analysis, the authority is in the Person
revealed rather than in the pages that do the revealing. This
does not lessen the authority of the Bible; it tremendously
increases it.

10

Pray

Prayer is not something to be added after other approaches in our search for the will of God have been tried and have failed. No, we should pray as we use the personal resources God has given us. Likewise, we should consider prayerfully the counsel we receive from others, and certainly we should always pray as we read and study the Bible.

Prayer and the will of God.—As is true of the reading and study of the Bible, we can derive both direct and indirect help from prayer. By direct help we mean that which comes in response to prayer regarding some particular decision or problem. The Bible plainly says, "If any of you falls short in wisdom, he should ask God for it and it will be given him, for God is a generous giver who neither refuses nor reproaches anyone" (James 1:5, *The New English Bible*). However, if one is to receive what he asks for he must ask "in sincere faith without secret doubts as to whether he really wants God's help or not" (James 1:6, Phillips). Do we not find here the reason why many of our prayers are not answered? We ask God to reveal his will to us, but sometimes down deep we do not want to know his will unless it coincides with our will.

It may sound contradictory to the preceding but our wills will not be brought into harmony with the will of God except through the spirit of genuine prayer. It was while Jesus prayed that he was transfigured (cf. Luke 9:29), was

69

clothed with the glory of the Father, a glory he had known before coming into the world. The glory of the Lord can become a reality in our lives only to the degree that our total personalities are possessed by him, only to the degree that his will becomes our will.

The preceding correctly implies that prayer will help us in indirect ways to understand more fully the will of our Heavenly Father. Prayer is not just asking God for something for ourselves or for others or even expressing our gratitude to him for his blessings. It is basically communication between God and man, and that communication does not consist exclusively or even primarily of words. It is a communion of spirits.

Jesus on occasions spent an entire night in prayer. Does this mean that he was pleading all that time with the Father for something? I think not. My judgment is that most of that time was spent in fellowship with the Father.

This kind of prayer or this phase of prayer, which might be a better way to express it, helps us in many indirect ways to see more clearly the purposes of God in our lives. It may include what has been called "creative silence" or "relaxed receptivity." It might be better to combine the two ideas and speak of "creative receptivity."

Prayer as communion is not necessarily silent or relaxed, although that aspect may and should be present. In an apparent but not a necessary contrast, some of the most dynamic, disturbing, and yet thrilling experiences that can ever come to a child of God is when he has been unusually conscious of the presence of the resurrected Christ. Such experiences do not come as frequently in any of our lives as they should. This may be one reason for our uncertainty concerning the will of God.

Prayer within the will of God.—John says, "This is the confidence which we have in him, that if we ask anything according to his will he hears us [will listen to us, Williams]" (1 John 5:14). Notice the "according to his will." Phillips translates this verse, "We have such confidence in him that we are certain that he hears every request that is made in accord with his own plan." Are our prayers in accord or in harmony with his will or plan?

It may be difficult or even impossible for us to know at times whether or not we are praying within the will of God. It is so easy for us to fool ourselves. Also, there are times when we cannot formulate our prayers in words. We seem not to know how to express the desires of our hearts. I am inclined to believe that the latter is true of most of our greatest experiences in prayer. Words seem to be an encumberance. Something within cries out to God. This may have been what Paul had in mind when he said, "We do not know how to pray as we ought" (Rom. 8:26). We do not know what to ask, nor how. We should be thankful, however, that "the Spirit comes to the aid of our weakness." He, "through our inarticulate groans," pleads for us and "God who searches our inmost being knows what the Spirit means, because he pleads for God's own people in God's own way" [according to the will of God, RSV]" (Rom. 8:26-27, *The New English Bible*). Here is both a glorious and potentially a terrible truth. It is glorious because we know that the Spirit can and does interpret our longings and even our imperfect attempts at prayer. It may be terrible because we cannot fool God. He does not listen primarily to the words we speak but to the deep desires of our souls. We may fool others and possibly even ourselves, but we cannot fool God. He knows whether or not we really want to know and do his will. Let us seek as best we can to "pray in the Holy Spirit" (Jude 20). When we do we can know that our prayers will be within the will of God and will be used and blessed by him to achieve his will in the world.

Prayer for the will of God.—We cannot, in the truest sense, pray within God's will without also praying for his will to be done. Let us, however, spell out this phase of prayer a little more specifically. We have not reached maturity in our prayer life until the main burden of our prayer is not for ourselves, not even that we may know and do God's will, but rather that his will may be done in our lives and also in our world. When we reach the latter stage in our praying we are then ready to be used by God in achieving his plan in and purpose for the world.

Jesus taught his disciples to pray, "Thy kingdom come, Thy will be done, in earth as it is in heaven (Matt. 6:10).

It is no mere accident that this is the first petition in the Model Prayer. George W. Truett used to say that no man has a right to pray, "Give us this day our daily bread," until he has first prayed, "Thy kingdom come, thy will be done." And if his will were done on earth as it is in heaven, his kingdom or his reign or rule would have come. In other words, here is one petition and not two. His kingdom comes as his will is done in our lives and in the world in which we live.

What we pray for, we are to work for. The two statements that stand so close together in the Sermon on the Mount, "Thy kingdom come" (a prayer), and "Seek first his kingdom" (Matt. 6:33), belong together. That which is to be the first petition in our prayers is also to be sought by us before all other things. Praying and working for the kingdom means praying and working for the purposes of God in the world.

As we mature in Christ, God's will, plan, purpose, reign, rule, or kingdom will increasingly be the unifying center of our prayers and of our lives in general. We shall more and more see the world in which we live from the perspective of our Heavenly Father.

The practice of prayer.—It will help a great deal as we seek to know the will of God if prayer becomes the practice of our lives. This will mean, among other things, that we shall have some regular prayer habits that have become fixed patterns in our lives. It should be just as unthinkable to start the day for the Lord without some time for communion with him as it would to begin the work of the day without our regular morning routine or preparation for the day. Likewise, at least a brief prayer should be a part of our preparation for retiring at night.

Perhaps you will want to combine Bible study and prayer. Such a period of devotion may be strictly private or you may join a friend, a roommate, or members of your family. Each will have his own particular plan and procedure, but to be sensitive to the will of the Lord in your life, cultivate his presence through *regular* Bible study and prayer.

The prayer life, however, of a mature Christian goes beyond these regular prayer habits. He discovers that increasingly he is conscious of the presence of the Lord as he goes about his daily tasks. He not only has fixed habits of prayer, which he still recognizes as important, but he also prays as he walks and talks, as he plays and works. He finds more and more that he can feel the touch of God's Spirit on his spirit as he breathes a prayer to God at most any time— day or night. This may be what Paul meant when he said, "Pray without ceasing" (1 Thess. 5:17, KJV), or "Pray constantly," or "Never stop praying" (Phillips). We pray constantly when we live in the atmosphere of prayer.

As we mature in prayer, we shall discover that we shall be more alert to and less uncertain about the will of God for our lives. We shall pray less for ourselves and more that God's will might be done in the world. Our conception of his will will become more inclusive. The maturing Christian also prays less that he may know the will of God and more that he may be used by the Lord to do his will in the world. In other words, he becomes less self-centered and more God-centered. Maturity in the Christian life is not necessarily related to age. Some of the most mature Christians are young in years.

The privacy of prayer.—Prayer in a group or with a prayermate or prayer partner may be quite meaningful, but prayer primarily is personal and private. It is basically the communion of the individual soul with God. Just before giving the Model Prayer, Jesus said to the disciples, "When you pray, go into a room by yourself, shut the door, and pray to your Father who is there in the secret place; and your Father who sees what is secret will reward you" (Matt. 6:6, *The New English Bible*). Jesus himself arose "a great while before day" and "went out to a lonely place, and there he prayed" (Mark 1:35). A place of real prayer is usually a lonely place, apart from others, even though others may be present. It is, however, in those lonely places, which do not mean necessarily geographic or even social isolation, that God speaks most distinctly to us.

It was in the garden of Gethsemane that Jesus left his disciples behind and went "a little farther," and there alone with God he accepted his Father's way and will for his life. It will be in the loneliness of "a garden experience" that many of you will be able to pray, "Not as I will, but as thou wilt." The discovery of, and particularly the submission to, the will of God is always a very personal experience.

11

Respond to the Holy Spirit

You will understand that there is no attempt in this chapter to discuss in general the nature or the functions of the Spirit, but merely to point out his relation to the will of God in our lives. The content of the chapter, in the main, could be summed up by saying that the child of God cannot know nor have the strength to do the will of God apart from the leadership of and the power that comes from the presence of the indwelling Spirit of God.

Our need for the Spirit.—Let us spell out a little more specifically our need for the Spirit's leadership and relate this need to the other resources we can use as we seek God's will for our lives. We may use to the fullest all of the personal resources God has given to us, and yet we will discover over and over again that we cannot know the will of God without the leadership of the Spirit of God.

We may seek the advice of the wisest and most skilled counselors, but unless they and we are led by the Spirit we shall usually find that we do not have a clear insight into the will of God. Even the Bible, God's message to us, will not give us the light we need unless its pages are illumined by the Spirit who inspired its writers. Also, we cannot pray as we ought except as the Spirit gives us utterance. We need his guidance in every decision.

You and I should be thankful to our Heavenly Father that the Holy Spirit has been given to us to dwell with us and within us (see John 14:17). We do not have to walk alone. When decisions must be made and when problems come we have one to stand by our side. This one knows the answers; he sees the way ahead. With our human limitations we may be mistaken about his leadership, but we can be sure that he is never mistaken about the way he wants to lead us.

The apostle Paul asks a question with an obvious answer. The question is, "Do you not know that you are God's temple and that God's Spirit dwells in you [has His home within you, Weymouth]?" (1 Cor. 3:16). Again Paul asks another question with a self-evident answer: "Do you not know that your body is a temple of the Holy Spirit within you, which you have from God [and the Spirit is God's gift to you, *The New English Bible*]?" (1 Cor. 6:19).

We have mentioned previously some of "God's good gifts." Will you not agree that God's best gift to us is the Spirit? As is true of all his best gifts, the Spirit is given to all his children. Since the Spirit has been given, we do not need to pray that the Spirit will come. He came in great power on the day of Pentecost. He has been present ever since that time. We do need to pray that we shall recognize his presence; and, most of all, we need to pray that God will help us to turn our lives over to his leadership. We can be sure that he will lead if we will follow.

What the Spirit can do.—Much of the work of the Spirit in our lives as children of God depends on our willingness to respond to the leadership of the Holy Spirit. God will not force his will and way on any child of his. He could not and be the kind of God he is and respect the kind of man he created. He does not want and he will not have unwilling slaves; he wants joyous, willing servants who will become partners with him in his work in the world.

This does not mean necessarily that God's Spirit cannot and does not perform any useful function in the lives of

God's children who are unwilling and rebellious. Some of us know by personal experience that when we wander from the way of God, when we are consciously outside his will, the Spirit works within us to convict us of our faults, our failures, our sins. He creates within us a deep unrest. He seeks to convince us of our need for his leadership, but it should be said again that he will never override our will. We can refuse to respond. In other words, we can say no to the Holy Spirit and make it stick. How much more glorious and blessed it would be for us and for the purposes of God in our lives and in our world, however, if we would say yes.

One of the functions of the Spirit in our lives is to lead us to a clearer understanding of the will of God and of the truth of God in general. This is seen in some statements Jesus made when he told his disciples about the coming of the Holy Spirit. In those marvelous addresses immediately preceding his crucifixion he spoke of "the Spirit of truth" (John 14:17,26; 15:26; 16:13-14), who was being sent to teach them "all things" or to guide them "into all the truth." The Spirit does not speak of himself or for himself but of and for the Father and the Son.

How the Spirit works.—If we want the leadership and the power of the Holy Spirit in our lives we must learn how to tarry or wait. We need to be still not only that we may know God (cf. Psalm 46:10) but also that we may know the will of God for our lives. We may become so active even in the work of the Lord that we do not have adequate time to be alone with him. Aloneness is an essential phase of our preparation for the leadership of the Spirit. He will not and cannot speak to or lead an unprepared heart. For many that preparation will take considerable time; for all it will require some time. Can and will we discipline ourselves to tarry or wait?

Jesus, after his resurrection, made some pointed statements to his disciples about waiting until the Spirit came. He told them to tarry or stay in Jerusalem until they were "clothed with power from on high" (Luke 24:49). After ten days of tarrying in prayer, that power came on the day of Pentecost when the Spirit descended upon the disciples. They could not have had the power of his presence without tarrying until his presence was made manifest among them.

Will you not agree that many times we stumble along in the dark, uncertain about the will of God in our lives and largely powerless in our work for God, because we have not taken the time to tarry until we have felt the touch of God's Spirit in our lives? And, many times that is a very light touch, or to change the figure of speech, he frequently speaks to us in "a still small voice" (1 Kings 19:12). We must be sensitive spiritually if we are to have his leadership.

"Walk by the Spirit."—"If we live by the Spirit, let us also walk by the Spirit" (Gal. 5:25). *The New English Bible* translates this verse, "If the Spirit is the source of our life, let the Spirit also direct our course," while Williams translates the last portion of the verse, "let us also walk where the Spirit leads." The life we have as Christians is the work of the Spirit. Since this is true, we should let him direct our course, or we should walk where he leads.

The context of this verse from Galatians reveals two marvelous results of walking where the Spirit leads or under the guiding impulse of the Spirit. One result is negative and the other positive. Both express the broader aspects of the will of God for our lives. Paul says, "If you are guided by the Spirit you will not fulfil the desires of your lower nature" (Gal. 5:16, *The New English Bible*). From the positive perspective he says, "But the fruit of the Spirit is love, joy, peace, patience, kindness, goodness, faithfulness, gentleness, self-control" (vv. 22-23). Here is God's standard of excellence for us. How do we measure up?

12

Have a Willing Heart

What are the things you want most in life—happiness, peace of mind, approval of parents, popularity, wealth, economic security, success? What would head your list?

Where would the will of God be on such a list? Would it be there at all? It should be at the top of the list for every child of God. There are not enough of us, older as well as younger, who put God's will first in our lives. We can all be sure that the depth and the sincerity of our desire to know and to do the will of God will largely determine the extent to which God will and can reveal his will to us.

Each of the divisions of this chapter will be developed on the basis of a verse of Scripture. Will you carefully and prayerfully study and meditate upon each one?

"If any man's will is to do his will, he shall know" (**John 7:17**).—If you will read the verses immediately preceding you will discover that Jesus was defending his teachings. He said that they were not his own but his Father's who had sent him. It was from that kind of a background that he said to the people in general but to the Jews in particular: "If anyone is willing to keep on doing God's will, he will know whether my teaching comes from God, or merely expresses my own ideas" (Williams).

Here is a basic principle that applies to the problem we have been discussing—how can we know the will of God? There is an affinity between the willing heart and the will of God. We can be sure that the more willing we are to do his will, the clearer and surer will be the revelation of his will to us. Many times we do not know the way we should go because we are not walking in the way of God now. Frequently we really do not want to know his will, or at least there are some mental reservations about doing his will. He cannot lead the unwilling heart.

Notice the verb tense in Williams' translation—"is willing *to keep on doing* God's will." This brings out the idea of continual action. When the doing of God's will has become the habit or the pattern of the individual's life, he will seldom have serious doubts for very long concerning the will of God for any area of his life. At least, he will have enough light, with rare exceptions, to take the next necessary step. The will of God tends to become the atmosphere of his life. He lives it and breathes it. Few of us have arrived at this stage.

"Be transformed . . . that you may prove what is the will of God" (Rom. 12:2).—Let us quote the entire verse from Williams: "Stop living in accordance with the customs of this world, but by the new ideals that mold your minds continue to transform yourselves, so as to find and follow God's will; that is, what is good, well-pleasing to Him, and perfect." *The New English Bible* suggests that when one's whole nature is transformed, he "will be able to discern the will of God, and to know what is good, acceptable, and perfect."

It is not our purpose to give a general interpretation to any of the Scriptures. However, two or three things in this verse from Romans are quite important from the viewpoint of our study.

The first admonition is, "Do not be conformed to this world." Williams translates this, "Stop living in accordance with the customs of this world." *The New English Bible* has it, "Adapt yourselves no longer to the pattern of this present world," and A. T. Robertson, in his *Word Pictures in the New Testament,* says, "Do not take this age as your fashion plate."

Does this not touch on a temptation that all of us have, but one that is particularly prevalent among young people? Even the nonconformists tend to conform to or live in accordance with the customs or mores of their own particular group. So nonconformity may be, in a sense, conformity.

Typical of the biblical emphasis in general, there is a positive as well as a negative exhortation in this Scripture verse. Paul admonishes us, as well as the Roman Christians, to be transformed. This transformation is through an inner renewal, which evidently refers to the new birth or the new man, which in turn is the work of the Holy Spirit.

The main emphasis in the verse, for the purpose of our study, is the results of the transformed life. This transformation, which itself is an expression of the will of God, makes it possible for us to discern, to know, to test, to prove, or to find and follow the will of God. The potential for the complete transformation of life is inherent in the initial experience when we become new creations in Christ Jesus. We can understand the will of God only to the degree that we let this potentiality become a reality in our lives. Notice that the progressive nature of this transformation is suggested by Williams' translation. It will not be complete until the end of life's journey; hence, we shall not know perfectly the will of God until we awake in his likeness. This should not discourage us; it should challenge us.

Only the individual whose mind has been renewed and whose life is in the process of being transformed can understand that the will of God is good, acceptable (Williams says "well-pleasing to Him"), and perfect. Phillips, in a charactertically free translation, says the following: "Let God remold your minds from within, so that you may prove in practice that the plan of God for you is good, meets all his demands and moves toward the goal of true maturity." Whether a correct translation or not, and all translations are interpretations to some degree, the ideas brought out so clearly by Phillips are true to Christian experience. As we let God reshape us from within, it is increasingly clear to us that his will and purpose is always good or best for us. Also, we see more and more clearly that following his plan or will for our lives moves us "toward the goal of true maturity."

"Knock, and the door will be opened" (Matt. 7:7, The New English Bible).—You recognize this as a part of that wonderful statement by Jesus in the Sermon on the Mount: "Keep on asking, and the gift will be given you; keep on seeking, and you will find; keep on knocking, and the door will open to you" (Williams).

Our Heavenly Father has good gifts he wants to give us, he has many doors he wants to open to us; but he will give those gifts and open those doors only if we persistently ask, seek, knock. This is the way of spiritual maturity for us. By waiting, seeking, knocking, our motives and purposes are examined and purified. We discover in the process some of the deeper truths of God. And when the door is opened and the gift is given, frequently there are riches beyond anything we ever anticipated. We would not have had the capacity to appreciate them had they been given or revealed without our seeking and knocking.

This verse of Scripture, on the surface, sounds contradictory to Revelation 3:20: "Behold, I stand at the door and knock; if any one hears my voice and opens the door, I will come in to him and eat with him, and he with me." Look again. Is there any real contradiction here? The evident answer is no. God responds to the seeking heart, but while he responds he also seeks. Does not his Holy Spirit prompt the asking, the seeking, the knocking?

Whatever may be the correct interpretation of this verse, I do not believe we do violence to it when we apply it to our own individual lives. He stands and knocks at the door of every human heart—Christian and non-Christian. For those of us who know him as Saviour and Lord, he wants into our lives more fully. He wants to live more completely within us. He wants to express himself more perfectly through us. Can you hear him knocking at the door of your own life?

Possibly most significant for our immediate purpose is the plain statement that we must open the door. He will knock, but the one on the inside must hear his voice and open the door. Just as he will not force his way into the life of the unsaved man, he will not force himself on those of us who are his children. He is a gentleman in the highest respect. He does not want to be and, in a sense, he will not be where he is not wanted.

Do you remember the famous painting of Christ at the door? I remember it from one of my readers in elementary school. It is said that when the artist had completed the picture a friend of his was looking at it. He commented favorably about the background, about the marvelous blending of colors, and particularly commended the clarity of the features of Jesus. Then he said, "But there is one thing lacking. There is no latch on the door."

The artist's reply was, "That is correct. The latch is on the inside of the door."

So it is with your heart and mine. We must open from within. Therefore, while we seek for the will of God, let us be sure to open our hearts as we feel his gentle knock. We can be sure that when we open the door he will come in, and when he comes in he will always bring abundant blessings to our lives, the greatest of which will be a sense of fellowship with him.

As we use our personal resources to seek for the will of God, let us be sure that we have a willing heart. Let the same be true as we counsel with others, as we read and study the Bible, as we pray, and as we seek the leadership of the Holy Spirit. It is only the seeking mind and the willing heart that can know the will of God. Obedience today will bring guidance tomorrow.

13

Look Beyond the Problems

You may still have some unanswered questions or unsolved problems concerning the will of God. Your search for the will of God will not be complete until you face up to and find at least a partial answer or solution for those questions or problems. These problems may tend to disturb or perplex you. If the latter is true it is not necessarily a sign of an unwilling heart or of spiritual immaturity. The three questions or problems we shall briefly consider are frequent sources of concern, if not perplexity, to even the most sincere and mature Christians.

God's will and our uncertainty.—We are not concerned here with uncertainties or doubts in general, but uncertainties concerning the will of God. There may be times when you utilize every available resource in your search for the will of God. So far as you can determine, you are willing to do his will; yet you are plagued with a lingering uncertainty. As positive a statement as you can make at such times is that you believe a particular thing to be his will, or you hope you are going in the direction he would have you go. If this has been or is your experience, let me assure you that most older Christians have frequently been where you are. They, at least occasionally, have had to feel their way. The steps they have taken have been with considerable hesitation. Such uncertainty may result in some painful soul-searching experiences.

It may be wise to suggest again, in a parenthetical paragraph, that sometimes we fail to see the way of the Lord clearly because down deep within us we are not entirely willing to do his will. There is an element of rebellion in our hearts. We need, over and over again, to pray that God will not only give us the light we need but that he will also give us the faith, the strength, and the courage we need to walk in that light. It is as impossible for us to do the will of God without his help as it is for us to know his will without his guidance.

Regardless of why we may be uncertain about the will of God, what can we do concerning our uncertainty? If the uncertainty relates to his will in the future, the answer is clear —we should wait patiently on the Lord. But what if the decision must be made? What if we stand at the forks of the road? Are we to stand still until the way is entirely clear? The obvious answer is no. Even if we would, we could not in many cases remain where we are. If we do not consciously and deliberately make a decision, the forces of life will frequently make it for us; they will pick us up and move us. Even indecision, under certain circumstances, will be a decision—at least a negative one.

What are we to do, however, about the uncertainty that remains? Let me make three or four suggestions to you that have been shared many times with young people through the years. They are a basic part of my conception of the Christian life. (1) When uncertainty is present, follow the best light you have. The light may be no more than a flicker or a speck, but follow it. You may have to step by faith, but step. (2) As you take the hesitant step, as you make your decision, ask God to give you the additional light you need or to block you if you are making a mistake. (3) Trust your Heavenly Father to keep you from going very far astray. You can do this if you are really willing to do his will.

Many older Christians can join me in saying that the preceding statements are in harmony with Christian experience. This does not mean, however, that we shall never make any mistakes. We are human; we are imperfect. The greatness of our God is proved, however, by his ability to take even our honest mistakes and weave them into the fabric of his design for our lives and for our world.

God's will, our will, and the will of others.—Have you ever known an individual who was quite sure that a particular thing was the will of God for his life, and yet it did not work out? Did this necessarily mean that he was wrong about the will of God; or is it possible that the fulfilment of the will of God in our lives may, at times, require more than our personal willingness? We must admit that it is possible for one to be wrong concerning the will of God, but the doing of God's will in our lives can be and frequently is determined by others. Let me suggest one very evident example.

It might be within the will of God for a particular couple to marry, but either one or both of them can thwart the purposes of God. So it is in many other areas of life. The achievement of the will of God in many situations requires the co-operation of all who are related in any way to the decision. Straight thinking regarding this whole matter may prevent some bitter, disillusioning experiences.

Let me pass on to you an illustration of the thing we have been talking about. A young minister had a deep conviction that God wanted him to be pastor of a particular church. The church did not call him, however, but turned to another. This resulted in a rather unhappy experience for both pastor and people. The minister himself later said that he was definitely outside of the will of God during his months with the church. When he resigned, the church did turn to the young minister who felt called, and he and the church were richly blessed during his five years as pastor.

Although I am not and never have been a pastor, I have had at least two experiences somewhat comparable to the young minister. I had a definite conviction that a certain thing was the will of God for my life, but it did not work out. It is possible, of course, that the young minister and I were mistaken about the will of God. None of us can escape the limitations of our humanity.

There are, however, at least three convictions that have resulted from my personal experiences and from my observation and knowledge of similar experiences in the lives of others. Sharing these convictions may be of help in some experience you may have in the days to come. (1) It is possible for individuals, agencies, or institutions to come between us and the will of God. (2) When we are willing to do our Father's will and through no fault of ours it does not work out, he will care for our interests. This is a glorious truth! When we seem to be blocked in doing the will of God, let us remember that our world has not totally collapsed. God is still on his throne watching over his own. (3) We can also be sure that God has a will for us in the new circumstances we face in life. We can have a rich and rewarding life of service for God and our fellowman. Sometimes this service will be so rewarding that we may wonder if our earlier conviction concerning the will of God was correct.

This is the logical place to mention again the distinction that Leslie Weatherhead has made between the ultimate, the intentional, and the circumstantial will of God. God's ultimate will is his big, over-all will, which is an expression of his sovereignty. It represents his basic redemptive purpose in the world; and no man, nation, or combination of men and nations can defeat him in its achievement. He will be triumphant in the world. He may lose some battles but he will not lose the war. God's intentional will might be equated with his ideal will or what has been called his perfect will. In contrast, his circumstantial will represents, in a sense, an adjustment of his perfect or intentional will to the immediate circumstances of life.

Do you see the relation of the preceding distinctions to the matter we have been discussing? Others may prevent our following or doing the perfect or intentional will of God. However, if we are faithful to God's circumstantial will we can be sure that our obedience will contribute, in some way and to some degree, to the achievement of his ultimate will.

God's will and human suffering.—The relation of God and his will to suffering and sorrow is one of life's most perplexing problems. Is all suffering and sorrow an expression of or in harmony with the will of God? You have possibly heard your pastor or some other minister say at a funeral: "The Lord gave, and the Lord has taken away; blessed be the name of the Lord." Is the Lord responsible for all deaths? If so, is he directly or indirectly responsible? What about the other sorrows of life—are they within the will of God? How can we explain the fact that some of God's best people suffer the most? The answers to these and related questions are not easy.

Here we are not talking primarily about the suffering that may result from doing the will of God. It has been suggested that God's will is always best for us and for his cause. This does not mean that it may not entail some suffering. Freedom from suffering cannot be equated with our best or our good.

The way of the Lord for our lives is not always smooth and pleasant. In following his will we may have to break with friends and even loved ones. We may suffer the loneliness that frequently is the lot of those who walk the high road of devotion to the purposes of God.

We may correctly believe that "it pays to serve Jesus," but we should also know that it costs to serve him, to walk in his way, to do his will. This should not surprise us, since Jesus himself, in response to the will of God, went through the garden of Gethsemane and up the hill of Calvary to the cross. We may be called upon to walk a similar route. Yet, underneath and beyond the suffering there can be a deep satisfaction and peace in knowing that we are within the will of God, and are being used by him as a redemptive influence in the lives of others.

Let us return to suffering in general, to suffering that does not come as a result of the doing of the will of God? What is the relation of the will of God to suffering in general, in the lives of non-Christians as well as Christians? This whole problem is so big and so involved that all we can do is to suggest at least a partial solution.

It seems quite evident that most suffering comes as a result of the operation of basic natural laws. God is the author of these laws, and he is responsible for most suffering only in the sense that he ordinarily permits the laws to function without interfering with them. A baby is born prematurely, is placed in an incubator, a nurse lets the incubator get too hot, and as a result the child has been physically and mentally handicapped all of his life. A law was violated and a certain result was inevitable. This means, among other things, that God did not in a miraculous way cause the child to be injured and, hence, bring an almost unbearable burden upon the parents. God would have had to work a miracle to prevent the child's injury. This tragedy was a part of God's circumstantial or permissive will but not an expression of his intentional, perfect, or ideal will.

It is not claimed that this is a full explanation for all suffering. We cannot prescribe or dictate the way God works. He is the source of the laws of life and is more powerful than those laws. It is true that he ordinarily lets them operate, but he may and does at times step into the process and makes the laws of life operate more effectively than they would otherwise. He also may and does set them aside at times. We can be relatively sure, however, that any time God steps in in some unusual way, he does so for the sake of a higher law. For example, when he sees fit in an unusual way to heal one he does this for a spiritual purpose. The latter implies that as a rule when God sees fit to step into the natural process in any unusual way, he does so to relieve rather than to cause suffering.

More important for us than an entirely adequate explanation for suffering is a proper attitude toward it when it comes. What will we let God do for us and to us in and through it? Suffering will never leave us the same. It will drive us farther away from or draw us closer to our Heavenly Father. It will embitter or sweeten our lives. It may become a self-defeating experience or a glorious triumph. Through suffering, we may feel more distinctly the heart beat of God. Regardless of why the suffering comes, our Heavenly Father would like to utilize it for his glory and our good.

Whether or not it is his will to remove the occasion for the suffering, it is always his will that we have peace of heart. The acceptance of what comes is the road to peace. It is also the way of victory. Paul prayed that the Lord would remove his thorn in the flesh. God did not remove the thorn, whatever it was, but he revealed to Paul that his grace would be sufficient (cf. 2 Cor. 12:7-9).

Our suffering can demonstrate the power of his grace. The author of Hebrews says that Christ "learned obedience in the school of suffering" (Heb. 5:8, *The New English Bible*) or "through what he suffered." He was also perfected through suffering (cf. Heb. 2:10). God, through our suffering, would teach us to obey, to co-operate with his will. Such submission or co-operation, in turn, is an essential phase of our spiritual maturing or perfection. In other words, God would use suffering in our lives to make us better men and women. This is seen in that great promise that has been a source of strength to many a suffering saint of God: "We know that all things work together for good to them that love God [who keep on loving God, Williams], to them who are called according to his purpose" (Rom. 8:28, KJV). That we might "be conformed to the image of his Son" (v. 29) is the purpose that God would achieve through the experiences of life, including suffering. This is what he wants to do for us. Will we let him?